Contents

Faith at Work

A Spirituality of Leadership

Donal Dorr

LITURGICAL PRESS
Collegeville, Minnesota

www.litpress.org

First published in 2006 as *Spirituality of Leadership* by The Columba Press, 55A Spruce Avenue, Stillorgan Industrial Park, Blackrock, Co Dublin.

Cover design by David Manahan, O.S.B.
Photo courtesy of Stockphoto.com.

Published in North America by Liturgical Press, Saint John's Abbey, P.O. Box 7500, Collegeville, Minnesota 56321-7500. www.litpress.org.

1	2	3	4	5	6	7	8

Library of Congress Cataloging-in-Publication Data

Dorr, Donal.
    Faith at work : a spirituality of leadership / Donal Dorr.
        p.   cm.
    Includes bibliographical references.
    ISBN-13: 978-0-8146-3182-9
    ISBN-10: 0-8146-3182-7
    1. Christian leadership.   2. Leadership--Religious aspects—Christianity.   3. Leadership--Religious aspects.   I. Title.
BV652.1.D67 2007
262'.1—dc22

                                         2006015515

Introduction

My aim in this book is to explore the nature of leadership and to outline a spirituality which can support authentic leadership. I am particularly concerned with how leadership is exercised in religious organizations of all kinds and in voluntary or nongovernmental agencies. However, I believe that much of the spirituality of leadership that I outline here would also be relevant in the business world as well as in the public services and in politics—if those in leadership roles there were willing to take it on.

I write out of my own background as a Catholic and a member of a missionary society. But the views I express here are also based on my experience of working with the leadership of many different religious congregations and agencies of my own church and other Christian churches, as well as with the management of voluntary groups and with management consultants. So I am confident that what I am saying is not just unrealistic theory but is based on practical experience.

The wider context in which I write is one where the issue of leadership has recently become a matter of considerable concern in the business world as well as in the Christian churches, in other religions, and in the political world. In the Catholic Church a crisis of leadership has been developing over the past generation. It has become more urgent with the election of Pope Benedict XVI who, prior to his election, was widely seen as somebody who exercised a quite authoritarian style of leadership. The

Anglican Church is going through a different kind of crisis of leadership. There are unresolved disagreements on moral and doctrinal issues between its different branches; and it seems that its leadership may not have sufficient authority to safeguard its unity. Meanwhile the leadership formerly exercised by the World Council of Churches is called in question by the growing power of Pentecostalism and of evangelical and fundamentalist Protestant churches. In Islam, the new dominance of Shia Muslims in Iraq and the emergence of Shia Iran as a major power give rise to serious issues about the political role of religious leaders.

In the political field, the West has been seeking to promote the development of democratic governments in the Middle East, and in the European and Asian countries that were formerly part of the Soviet bloc, as well as in many of the so-called developing countries in Africa and Latin America. This has given rise to much skepticism since many people hold that the word democracy has been devalued. They believe it has come to be equated with a form of government that is pro-Western in a political sense, and is also committed to economic policies that leave these countries at the mercy of a process of globalization that benefits Western-based transnational companies. Furthermore, the increasing incidence of terrorism has led even the leaders of democratic governments to adopt repressive measures that threaten people's fundamental human rights. The question arises whether countries everywhere can find leaders who will have both the vision and the support to find an alternative. What is required is a model of governance that will ensure an adequate measure of security, while respecting fundamental human rights and finding a way to ensure that alienated minorities play a constructive role in society.

In this book I am not directly addressing these global issues of authority and leadership. I am writing primarily for those who are called to exercise leadership in much smaller arenas. Nevertheless, the material also has a relevance for the wider global issues. This is because part of the challenge for leaders of relatively small-scale voluntary agencies and religious organizations today is to provide a model of how leadership should be exercised.

The book begins with a short chapter in which I pick out certain key passages in the Bible that provide a basis for a Christian spirituality of leadership. In the following two chapters I look at various spiritualities that have been significant in the history of the Christian church. These provide the background against which we can develop a spirituality of leadership appropriate for our time. My account of these different spiritualities of leadership and authority brings out the fact that there is a strong and consistent democratic tradition within Christianity—and even in the Catholic Church, which is often seen as having a quite authoritarian structure.

This ancient and enduring democratic spirituality is far more profound than the simplistic version of democracy being used— and frequently misused—in the Western world at present and that the United States government is attempting to export to other parts of the world. Rather it is one that takes freedom of personal choice very seriously and respects the sacredness of conscience.

The understanding of authority and leadership that permeates the spirituality of the major religious orders in the Catholic Church and some strands in the Protestant tradition is one that takes it for granted that the Holy Spirit speaks to each individual, providing guidance to anybody who is prepared to listen. Furthermore, it assumes that the Spirit provides guidance to whole communities and congregations, leading them into a deeper understanding of their faith and inviting them to relinquish out-of-date attitudes and practices and to step bravely into challenging new ministries.

This understanding of personal and corporate guidance has obvious implications for what is involved in leadership. It puts the emphasis on the dialogue of the Spirit with individuals and whole communities, rather than on the kind of maintenance tasks that tend to occupy most of the time and energy of many of those who were elected or appointed to give leadership. Of course the task of leaders includes maintaining order, filling the existing job vacancies, and ensuring that all the members of the group do their work and are reasonably content in doing so. But something more is required. Leadership is fully authentic only when it is exercised by those who are inspired and inspiring. But they must at the same time be willing to recognize the wisdom and inspiration of others. And they must be able to work with others toward a common vision that unites and inspires a whole community.

Within this ancient Christian democratic and Spirit-inspired tradition there are different approaches, giving a wide variety in the manner in which leadership is exercised in practice. For instance, the Dominican tradition in the Catholic Church and the Congregational tradition among Protestants, value a decentralized approach. The Ignatian tradition, on the other hand, uses a highly centralized model of authority, combined with an emphasis on personal and corporate discernment. But such differences should not distract us from what all these spiritualities of authority and leadership have in common. Nor should they allow us to overlook the challenge they pose to the way authority is exercised at present in most business enterprises as well as in the Catholic Church by Rome, by most bishops, and by many of our pastors on the ground. The contrast between the two styles of leadership has been growing wider in recent centuries and is particularly evident at the present time.

The leaders and members of religious orders and churches where the traditional democratic models of governance are practiced have much to teach the sectors of the church where a more authoritarian style of leadership is practiced. They also have a mission to the wider society that is in sore need of more effective, more sophisticated, and more respectful models of leadership than we find in the global and local political world of today.

However, the leaders of these congregations, societies, and churches do not have all the answers. They themselves have much to learn from political philosophers and management consultants who may have little or no connection with the church. In chapters 4, 5, and 6 of this book I have drawn on the thinking and accumulated wisdom of some of these scholars and practitioners to suggest approaches that may be of benefit to those in a leadership role in church and volunteer organizations.

The heart of this book comes in chapters 7, 8, and 9 where, drawing on all that has gone before, I put forward my own views. In chapter 7, I outline some key elements of authentic leadership. Then I describe different kinds of leader, which I call the *lone leader,* the *emergent leader,* the *classic leader,* and the *power-hungry leader.* In the eighth chapter I go on to outline five styles or manners in which good leadership is exercised, ranging from the empowerment style to the inspiring style. I believe each of these styles is appropriate in different situations and that all of them are necessary if leaders today are to be both respectful and effective. Chapter 9 looks closely at the role of vision in the exercise of leadership.

In the final four chapters I spell out in more detail some of the ways leadership is exercised in practice. Chapter 10 offers some practical guidelines and suggestions that those in leadership roles may find helpful. In chapters 11, 12, and 13, I look closely at one of the key issues for leadership, namely, techniques of individual and communal discernment. Starting with the Ignatian approach to discernment, I go on to explore the role of intuition in discernment and decision making. The appendix deals with a rather technical issue that has practical implications: the nature of consolation without cause and how it may relate to intuition.

In writing this book I have drawn both on written materials and on my own experience. Thirty years ago I became involved in leadership training, and it has taken up a sizable portion of my life ever since then. For over twenty years my work was mainly in what is called capacity building. This means that I was involved in facilitating training workshops for community activists and would-be leaders. In more recent years my focus has switched mainly to facilitating workshops for the leadership teams of religious congregations and of nongovernmental organizations. In these workshops I have been concerned not so much with the day-to-day practical issues of management but rather with helping the participants to develop their creativity, their intuitive powers, and their relationships with each other.

All during this period I was also engaged in research and writing about issues of social justice, mission, and spirituality. This provided a background for the leadership workshops in which I was involved. It is only very recently that it occurred to me that I might write a book about the spirituality of leadership. Early in 2005 I was invited by the staff of The Religious Formation Ministry Programme (Loreto House) in Dublin to take a seminar-workshop module on leadership as part of their yearlong program. Shortly afterwards I was invited to give input on the same topic to the central leadership team of my own missionary society, St. Patrick's Missionaries (Kiltegan). These requests provided a stimulus for me to begin writing on the topic, drawing on my experience and doing some further research. Almost before I knew it, what I was writing had grown into the size of a book. So I decided to revise and further expand it, and to have it published in the hope that it may be of some benefit to a wider audience.

My hope is that this book will be of interest first of all to Christians who hold leadership roles in various kinds of organizations—religious congregations, missionary societies, and programs or institutions related to health, community organizing, social action, and informal or formal education. I would like to think it may also have something to say to those who have a leadership or management role in the business world as well as to bishops, priests, pastors, and even to the top authorities of the Christian churches; perhaps also to those who exercise authority in governmental agencies and in the strictly political world. I have adopted an explicitly Christian approach to the topic. But I believe that those who are interested in spirituality, even if they do not share my Christian faith, should find that most of the material is also relevant to their situation.

This book is not intended to cover the day-to-day management issues that arise in running any organization. There are plenty of books about management. What I think is needed is material on leadership—and particularly on the spirituality of leadership. That is what I have tried to offer here.

I am grateful to those who shared insights with me or put me in touch with resources on various traditions of spirituality: Geraldine Smyth, Tom Jordan, and Bernard Treacy on the Dominican approach, Barbara Linen and Claire Murphy in relation to Cornelia Connelly, Cecelia Goodman and Pat Murray on Mary Ward's understanding of authority, Brian O'Leary, s.j., and Noel Bradley on the Ignatian tradition, and Sean Collins for providing me with material that I have used almost verbatim on Francis of Assisi. I am particularly grateful to my brother Frank and my sister-in-law Eileen Lynch for enlightenment and many hours of dialogue about discernment, and to my friend and colleague Pádraig Ó Máille for his rigorous reading of earlier drafts and his very helpful suggestions, particularly in relation to the concept of inspiring leadership and to my treatment of discernment.

Donal Dorr
September 2005

Chapter 1

Biblical Aspects

In this chapter I propose to look briefly at some passages from the Old Testament and the New Testament to see what light they throw on the concepts of authority and leadership.

Old Testament

One of the most important things we can learn about leadership from the Old Testament is that it comes as a call from God. We see this already in the call of Abraham (Gen 12:1) and it becomes very clear in the call of Moses: "I am sending you to Pharaoh, for you to bring my people the Israelites out of Egypt" (Exod 3:10).

The person who is called by God to be a leader feels incompetent or unworthy. Moses responded, "Who am I to go to Pharaoh?" (Exod 3:11) and later, "I have never been eloquent . . . for I am slow and hesitant of speech" (Exod 4:10). In fact God seems to deliberately choose unlikely people whom neither they themselves nor others would have thought of as natural leaders. This was the case when God told Samuel that Saul was the chosen one. Saul said, "Am I not a Benjaminite, from the smallest of the tribes of Israel? And is not my family the least of all the families of the tribe of Benjamin?" (1 Sam 9:21). It was even more striking in the case of the choosing of David, the son who had not even been presented to Samuel: "There is still one left, the youngest; he is looking after the sheep" (1 Sam 16:11). It is significant, however, that once these unlikely people have been chosen and anointed they become inspired and inspiring leaders and their people begin to see in them the leadership qualities that had not previously been evident.

Needless to say, we cannot interpret these passages in a fundamentalist way to draw any immediate conclusions about leadership today. But they do suggest two interesting ideas. The first is that a call to leadership, if it is authentic, is experienced as having a certain transcendent quality to it. For the Christian believer this means that even though the call is mediated through the humans who elected or selected the new leader, nevertheless the call comes from God. And this should not be just a matter of blind faith. The chosen leader should also experience this in some degree. Furthermore, the group or community should have some sense that this new leader has been chosen by God and given to them as a gift from God. Of course some members may find themselves surprised at, or even somewhat resistant to, this gift; but they should work to open up within themselves a space of welcome for the new leader.

A second idea suggested by the passages from the Old Testament is that we should be prepared to look for our leaders not just among the best-known and most obvious candidates. It may be that God expects us to play a role similar to the one played by the prophet Samuel—not simply to go by purely human calculation but to look more widely and listen for, and expect, the inspiration of God in the choice of leaders. And we should be willing to allow our leaders to grow into the role that has been given to them, as Moses and Saul and David did.

Perhaps the most striking text on leadership in the Old Testament comes when Solomon becomes king and God asks what gift he wants:

> Solomon replied, "Yahweh my God, you have made your servant king in succession to David my father. But I am a very young man, unskilled in leadership. . . . So give your servant a

> heart to understand how to govern your people, how to discern
> between good and evil, for how could one otherwise govern
> such a great people as yours?" It pleased Yahweh that Solomon
> should have asked for this. "Since you have asked for this," God
> said, "and not asked for long life for yourself or riches or the
> lives of your enemies but have asked for a discerning judgment
> for yourself, here and now I do what you ask. I give you a heart
> wise and shrewd as no one has had before and no one will have
> after you" (1 Kgs 3:6-12).

The significant point here is that the kernel of leadership is
not simply the power to influence people or the ability to provide effective and efficient governance. Rather the gift of wise
leadership has to do above all with moral issues. It is the ability
"to discern between good and evil." This is where the biblical
position contrasts sharply with that of Machiavelli—and with
the attitude of many who hold leadership positions in today's
world.

New Testament

Probably the most commonly quoted passage of Scripture that
refers to authority is from the letter to the Romans:

> Everyone is to obey the governing authorities, because there
> is no authority except from God and so whatever authorities
> exist have been appointed by God. So anyone who disobeys an
> authority is rebelling against God's ordinance; and rebels must
> expect to receive the condemnation they deserve. . . . You must
> be obedient . . . not only because of . . . retribution, but also
> for conscience's sake. (Rom 13:1-2, 5)

This text provides a basis for the legitimacy of civil governments. But it has often been misused to inculcate unquestioning
obedience, and even to suggest that people should put up with
abuses of power by oppressive authorities. Properly understood,
of course, it simply means that the civil authorities should be
obeyed unless their demands go against one's conscience. The

text may be linked to the passage from the First Epistle to Timothy indicating that the task of civil authorities is to ensure that the citizens can live in peace and mutual respect: "I urge then, first of all that petitions, prayers, intercessions and thanksgiving should be offered for everyone, for kings and others in authority, so that we may be able to live peaceful and quiet lives with all devotion and propriety" (1 Tim 2:1-2).

Far more significant texts about authority and leadership are found in the gospels. We can begin with this striking passage from St. Matthew's Gospel:

> Jesus called his followers together and said: "You know that the kings of the heathen lord it over their people and dominate them. That is not the way you are to exercise authority. Any of you who wants to be great must be the servant of the others; and the one who wants to be first among you must become your slave." (Matt 20:25-27)

This passage needs no explanation or commentary. It is a straightforward invitation from Jesus to any of his followers who takes up a leadership or authority role to take it on, not for personal power or honor, but purely as an act of service.

The same theme comes up again three chapters later in the same gospel: ". . . you are not to be called rabbi . . . call no one on earth your father. . . . The greatest among you will be your servant. All who exalt themselves will be humbled" (Matt 23:8-12).

In an interesting article Wilfrid Harrington points out that Jesus "stood authority on its head: *exousia* (authority) is shown to be *diakonia* (service)." The reason Jesus insisted that nobody on earth should be given the titles "rabbi" or "father" was that he saw genuine religion as "characterized by simplicity, affection, brother/sisterhood"; so "there ought not be an insistence on privilege and an exercise of power that distort this relationship." Harrington notes that Matthew's treatment of this topic is very strong because, by the time the gospel was being written, "Christian leaders were sporting title and flexing ecclesiastical muscle" (Harrington 2005, 51–2).

In regard to the use of power, Jesus himself showed the way. The gospel passages that describe his temptations (Matt 4:1-10 and Luke 4:3-13) indicate that the primary temptation was in regard to how he would use his power. He was being tempted to present himself as a wonder-worker (changing stones into bread), as somebody who could defy the law of gravity (jumping from the Temple). So he would be using his power to impress and overawe people to such an extent that they would effectively be powerless to oppose him. Seeing this as a temptation to use his human power abusively, he rejected it. He insisted that it is only to God that we should submit ourselves unconditionally. The authentic road for Jesus—and for us who follow him—is to leave people free to accept or reject him.

A key passage about leadership is from St. John's account of the Last Supper:

> Jesus . . . got up from the table, took off his outer robe, and tied a towel around himself. Then he poured water into a basin and began to wash the disciples' feet and to wipe them with the towel that was tied around him. . . . After he had washed their feet, had put on his robe, and had returned to the table, he said to them, "Do you know what I have done to you? You call me Teacher and Lord—and you are right, for that is what I am. So if I, your Lord and Teacher, have washed your feet, you also ought to wash one another's feet. For I have set you an example, that you also should do as I have done to you. Very truly, I tell you, servants are not greater than their master, nor are messengers greater than the one who sent them." (John 13:3-5, 12-16)

This passage, like those from St. Matthew's Gospel, stresses the role of service. But, as Raymond Brown points out (1970, 564), there is a further and deeper meaning. Even slaves were not required to wash the feet of their owner, but occasionally disciples would wash the feet of their master as a sign of their devotion. So the washing by Jesus of the feet of his disciples was a special act of love. What Jesus is asking, then, is that those who are in a role of leadership or authority should not merely provide service to others but should do so in a spirit of exceptional devotion and love.

A fourth key passage in the gospels about leadership comes in St. John's Gospel account of the postresurrection meeting of Peter with Jesus:

> Jesus said to Simon Peter, "Simon son of John, do you love me more than these others do?" He answered, "Yes, Lord, you know I love you." Jesus said to him, "Feed my lambs." A second time he said to him, "Simon son of John, do you love me?" He replied, "Yes, Lord, you know I love you." Jesus said to him, "Look after my sheep." Then he said to him a third time, "Simon son of John, do you love me?" Peter was hurt that he asked him a third time, "Do you love me?" and said, "Lord, you know everything; you know I love you." Jesus said to him, "Feed my sheep. In all truth I tell you, when you were young you put on your own belt and walked where you liked; but when you grow old you will stretch out your hands, and somebody else will put a belt round you and take you where you would rather not go." In these words he indicated the kind of death by which Peter would give glory to God. After this he said, "Follow me." (John 21:15-19)

The most important point here is that love is the primary quality Jesus looks for in a leader (cf. Brown 1970, 1111). Peter has made mistakes. He has been impetuous and hot-headed. He has denied his Master. But all this can be overlooked because he has love.

Of course what Jesus asks of Peter is love for Jesus himself and not explicitly for the flock. But, as Brown (1115) points out, the total devotion of Peter to Jesus means that Jesus can safely entrust his flock to Peter. There are interesting implications when this is applied to those who hold any leadership role in the church today. First of all, leadership should only be entrusted to a person who is loving to a high degree. Second, the Christian leader's love is first of all for Jesus; but then it is put into practice by committed love for the "flock" or community.

Another important implication of this passage is that the flock or community belongs to Jesus, and not to the leader (v. 16: "look after my sheep"). Leaders are not entitled to imagine that they "own" the community. By constantly thinking of the community as "the followers of Jesus" rather than as "my people" the leader can avoid many of the typical faults of leaders, such as being too controlling, or feeling unduly responsible either for the welfare of the group or for the mistakes or inadequacies of individuals in the group or of the group as a whole.

An important lesson can be drawn from the later part of this passage. It is that leaders who follow in the way of Jesus can expect to suffer. They will find they are no longer free to go in the way they would have wished. They are often compelled to do things and put up with treatment they would not have willingly chosen. The biblical writer sees this passage as a reference to the kind of death Peter had to undergo. But, as we apply it today, it can refer to a more drawn-out kind of martyrdom—that of the leader who is pressured from above by higher authorities and from below by the insistent demands of the community; or it could be applied to the martyrdom of the leader who is scapegoated by some or all of the members of the community.

Chapter 2

The Christian Tradition

For the first three hundred years of its existence, the church remained on the margins of society and at times the Christians were severely persecuted. Things changed dramatically when Constantine adopted Christianity as the official religion of the Roman Empire. Before long, church leaders began to take on some of the imperial trappings of honor and power.

This created serious problems in regard to both the exercise and the spirituality of authority and leadership—problems that have endured right up to the present time. From a fairly early stage, however, the religious orders provided an alternative way of looking at authority—one that is much closer to what we find in the Scriptures and especially in the example of Jesus. For this reason I will focus mainly, in this chapter, on the contribution of the founding figures of some of the great religious orders.

The Benedictine Model

We can begin by looking at the Benedictine model of leadership, worked out by St. Benedict who lived in the years from 480 to 543. At its core is the idea that the abbot is a father figure as one who can serve the community (and presumably the abbess is mother). In his Rule, St. Benedict says of the abbot: "His goal must be profit for the monks, not pre-eminence for himself" (ch. 64 cited in Bowman 2004, 77). There is a vow of obedience to the abbot, but this does not mean that the members of the community are seen as children. In fact there is communal ownership of the property, the abbot is elected for a fixed period by the professed members of the community, and major decisions are taken not by the abbot but collectively by the professed members of the community; on less major issues the abbot has to work with his council (Bowman, 65–78).

Anthony Marett-Crosby (in Dollard 2002, 48–58) notes that Benedict uses four images for the role of the abbot. First, he is to be close to Christ and to inspire others to come close to Christ; so in some sense he takes the role of Christ, above all in his role of service. Second, he is the shepherd, adapting with understanding to the needs of each member of the community, rather than imposing the same demands on everybody; and he must have a particular concern for "the lost sheep." Third, he has the role of healer, one who knows how to heal his own wounds and those of others; and he is to recognize the healing gifts others in the community have and to share his healing role with them. Finally, he is also the steward, that is, one who has a responsibility for the property of the monastery and community. However, he is to exercise this stewardship mainly by delegating it to others. Benedict wants the abbot to leave the management of the practical and material side of the monastery to other functionaries, allowing the abbot to focus on the spiritual welfare of the community and its members.

The Franciscan Model

St. Francis and St. Claire provided inspiration and a focus for numerous men and women who opted to follow them in living a life of radical poverty and simplicity. Francis founded his order in 1209. In the Franciscan tradition the leader is a minister, that is, the servant of the community. At the heart of the ideal of Francis was his desire that his brothers be *minores*, little people, and *fratres,* brothers to all. He wrote in the first rule, "Let none of them be called prior, but let all be called simply lesser brothers. And let them wash one another's feet" (Earlier Rule 6:3 quoted in Collins 2005).

Authority for Francis is the authority of the Holy Spirit, who inspired the brothers to embrace the life of the gospel. He built his order on the belief that each individual brother is led by the Spirit; and that the fraternity as a whole is collectively guided by the Spirit in living the gospel. In fact, Francis wanted to put in the rule that the true minister general of the order is the Holy Spirit.

Francis took the notion of authority as service very literally. He insisted that friars who come to their ministers (i.e., the local leaders) because they were having difficulty in keeping the rule according to the Spirit, are to be welcomed with great love and kindness. The Final Rule went on to say that the ministers must be so approachable that the other members of the community treat them as if they were servants—"for this is how it should be, that the ministers be the servants of all the brothers" (Final Rule 10:6–7, Collins).

The biggest fear Francis had in regard to the exercise of authority was that the ministers might give in to the temptation to inject their own agenda between the Holy Spirit and the brothers. In one of his surviving letters he urged a minister never "to demand that they [the brothers] be better Christians, just to suit your convenience, than the Lord gives them grace to be" (Letter to a Certain Minister 6–7, Collins).

The strongest criticism of Francis was for the minister who wants to cling to office: "if he gets more upset at having his office taken away than he would at being removed from the task of washing feet, then he is surely laying up treasure for himself and imperilling his soul" (Admonition 4:3, Collins).

The views of Francis about authority were worked out partly in dialogue with Claire; and the women in the Franciscan tradition live according to the same ideals as the men. There is, however, one further point that is significant in Claire's approach. It is resistance to undue interference by those who hold high office in the church. Claire resisted the determined attempt of the church authorities to force her sisters to follow the existing practice in relation to ownership of property; she insisted on a more radical approach to the practice of poverty.

In the years and decades after the time of Francis, there were many different understandings of his inspiration and charism, particularly on the issues of poverty and authority. Some of those who claimed to be Franciscans adopted such anarchic views that they were perceived as a threat to the authority of both church and state. This led to a condemnation of the more extreme views and practices, and to a tightening up of the authority and leadership structures of the Franciscan order.

The Dominican Model

Just nine years after the foundation of the Franciscan Order, St. Dominic founded his Order of Preachers. His approach to leadership was similar in some respects to that of Francis. But where the original Franciscan style was quite charismatic and unstructured, Dominic deliberately designed a structure—one that is quite radically democratic. For him wisdom resides in the community rather than mainly in its leader. In the Dominican way of thinking the prior or prioress is seen as "first among equals" rather than as a father figure or mother figure.

In 1220 Dominic convened the first general chapter of his order. It was composed of the representatives of the dozen priories in existence at that time. There he deliberately submitted himself to the judgment of the group and allowed them to reject his view on some important issues. As Malachy O'Dwyer says, Dominic shared his vision and his inspiration with others but allowed them "to make it their own and give it a shape that is to their own liking" (O'Dwyer 2003, 217, cf. 222).

Ever since the time of Dominic there have been regular and frequent general chapters of the order where the leadership is held accountable to the delegates. Furthermore, there is a whole variety of provincial or regional chapters or gatherings where policy is decided. This democratic approach extends right down to the level of the local community. It is the community as a whole that makes policy decisions; and the prior or leader of the community is not appointed by a higher authority but is elected by the members of that community. This means that what we find in the Dominican tradition is democracy from the ground up. There are quite severe limits to the authority of the master general; he does not have day-to-day executive power, apart from some special situations (Mills 1983, 187).

The basic principle behind this democratic approach was, and still is, a conviction that each member of the community is to be respected and valued. The former master general, Timothy Radcliffe, maintained that the best part of being in a leadership role was not the imposition of one's own ideas but discovering "the richness of the brethren" (O'Dwyer 2003, 223). In the Dominican tradition a diversity of views is not merely allowed for but is really valued. The resulting pluralism is a source of tension—especially since at times it arises from the imperfections and shortcomings of some of the members. Nevertheless, it is seen as an enrichment and a blessing (O'Dwyer 227). To respect others is to respect their freedom.

> Freedom is our birthright. To deny it to others is to deny them their vocation. Nor should we be tempted in times of stress or crisis to sacrifice or curtail this freedom for the sake of expediency or efficiency. (O'Dwyer 229)

The genius of Dominic was that he devised a structure that respected the value of individual freedom, while at the same time safeguarding the survival and flourishing of both the local communities and the order as a whole. A very large part of the Dominican constitutions is concerned with the governance of the order. The constitutions, as John Orme Mills points out, are full of checks and balances (Mills 1983, 185). Time and again, Dominicans emphasize the importance of their constitutions and their overall legal structure and tradition.

At the present time when many people see structures as opposed to freedom, it is interesting and thought-provoking to have a group who value their legal structure as a protection for the freedom of the individual. However, it must be added at once that those in the Dominican tradition do not imagine that what they have inherited is a legal blueprint, valid for all times and circumstances. It is rather "a complex organization requiring constant attention, re-evaluation and adjustment" (O'Dwyer 226).

One of the most radical innovations of Dominic was that he broke with tradition by insisting that those in leadership roles should hold office only for a fixed time period rather than for life. By doing so he established a truly important precedent. The electing of leaders for a fixed period is one of the most important ways in which authority and leadership are exercised in religious congregations and societies in contrast to the practice in the hierarchical church; and it helps to account for the wide gap that exists at present between the two.

The Reformation

One of the key factors in the Protestant Reformation of the sixteenth century was a rejection of what was seen as the undue power of priests, bishops, and the Pope. In the different Protestant churches and sects there emerged a wide variety of authority structures and conceptions of leadership. What all of them had in common was a deliberate commitment to put limits to clerical power.

The Society of Friends, popularly called the Quakers, have virtually no authority structures at all; they are, however, very loyal to certain traditional practices and values through which they retain their identity. Quite a number of the churches of the Reformation have congregational structures where authority is very decentralized at every level from local to international. The Church of England has worked out a carefully balanced structure in which authority at the national level is shared out between the bishops and representatives of the clergy and of the laity. Most of the larger Protestant churches have somewhat similar structures. The Anglicans and the Protestants also endeavor to keep a balance between the desire for a fair measure of local autonomy and the need for some central authority that can speak and act on behalf of the church as a whole—at least at the national level, and sometimes at the international level as well.

The effect of these less hierarchical authority structures is that leadership is more diffuse than in the Catholic Church. The higher authority roles in these churches may be largely nominal and ceremonial. Those who hold these roles may have little actual power to get things done. Indeed they often see themselves as conciliators who have no wish to impose their own views on others—and they may have been chosen for this very reason.

This has significant implications in relation to the exercise of leadership. It means that quite frequently the really effective leaders in these churches are strong, committed, charismatic people who occupy places lower down the line in the formal authority structures. There is quite a contrast in this regard between the Anglican and Protestant churches on the one hand and the Catholic Church on the other. Those who occupy authority roles in the Catholic Church have access to real power. At times some of those who have such ecclesiastical power have used it to stifle leadership that may be emerging from below.

The Ignatian Model of Leadership

Three hundred years after the time of Francis and Dominic the situation in the church in Europe had changed radically. The new situation was mainly a result of the Protestant Reformation, but it was also partly due to colonial expansion. In response to the challenge of the times, Ignatius Loyola devised a radically new type of religious order. The Jesuits were founded in 1539 and approved by the Pope in the following year. A different conception of authority and leadership was central to this new approach.

Prior to the time of Ignatius the church had three main models of authority. The bishop and the Pope saw themselves as princes of the church. The Benedictine abbot was intended to be a kindly spiritual father-figure. The leaders of the Franciscan and Dominican friars set out not to be above the members of their communities but to take a service role and to be, at most, first among equals. The Ignatian concept of authority differs significantly from all three of these. It combines two key elements: a highly centralized (almost military) authority structure and a strong emphasis on personal discernment.

Ignatius wanted the leader of his order to be a general in the literal sense, somebody who had authority to move his members anywhere in the world at short notice. This approach is encapsulated in the oft-quoted telegram allegedly sent to a Jesuit: "Go Jamaica Monday." The purpose behind this military-style discipline was not, of course, to glorify the general. One view of the aim of Ignatius was that it was to provide "New Athletes to combat God's enemies," and that this involved putting a halt to the progress of the Reformation (Wright 2005, 13). A less tendentious description of the purpose of the Jesuits was that it was to propagate the gospel and serve the church by responding quickly and effectively to the needs of the time as perceived by the leader in consultation with his close associates.

From this point of view the members of the order could be seen as commandos in the army of Jesus, ready to go anywhere and do anything that would serve the cause. But, though there is a certain validity in this commando image, it can also be quite misleading. For the followers of Ignatius were not trained to do just one task. The different members could take on very different ministries; and many of them were qualified for a variety of different kinds of work. In this situation the task of the overall leader was not just to fit all the members into one single mold. On the contrary, it was to discern the gifts of the very different individuals in the order and to ensure that these talents were developed, honed, and used in the ways that would best serve the mission.

The military-style discipline of the Ignatian approach to leadership was balanced by a strong commitment to personal discernment. In the Ignatian model of discernment the issue that is to be decided is explored not just in a purely rational-discursive manner. Prayer is brought very explicitly into the process of personal decision making; and a prominent role is given to feelings of consolation or desolation in the whole process of discernment.

On at least two important occasions Ignatius and his first companions used a process of communal discernment (Futrell 1970a, 122–3). There are fairly good indications of the kind of process they used. However, Ignatius did not lay down a detailed set of rules for a formal process of communal discernment, analogous to his rules for personal discernment. It was only from 1970 onward, with the renewal of Ignatian spirituality, that serious attempts were made to work out the details of a structured form of communal discernment. I will give a much fuller account of the Ignatian approach to discernment in chapters 11 and 13 and in the appendix to this book.

The approach of Ignatius has been hugely influential. Very many of the religious congregations and societies founded after his time adopted his model of mission, spirituality, and leadership. But it is interesting to note that, right up to the time of Vatican II, most of them bought into the Ignatian style of quasi-military discipline, while failing to take very seriously the concept of discernment.

The undervaluing of the key element in Ignatian discernment had already begun shortly after the death of Ignatius. The Jesuits' Official Directory of 1599 made a significant shift: its authors played down the importance of discernment on the basis of feelings, giving priority instead to a more rational style that Ignatius had seen as a kind of fall-back approach when the other one failed.

The playing down of the importance of spiritual feelings was linked not only to an excessive emphasis on the power of reason, but more particularly to an emphasis on the role of authority. This change of emphasis is understandable in the light of the situation of the church at the time, when the church leaders felt threatened both by Protestantism and by a kind of illuminism where some people claimed to be led by the Spirit with no reference to external authority. Nevertheless it had unfortunate consequences. It gave rise to a situation where, in the period between the Council of Trent four hundred years ago and Vatican II forty years ago, most religious congregations developed a very authoritarian model of leadership; and the associated spirituality emphasized that the will of the superior is the voice of God.

This insistence on obedience at the expense of personal discernment and conviction came despite the witness of several of the great founding figures of these religious congregations. Take for instance Mary Ward who in 1609 founded a religious institute to which both the Loreto Sisters and the Congregation of Jesus (until recently called the IBVM) trace their origin. She was quite sure that she was led by God in making key decisions. Even when she met the Pope she did not ask him to tell her what she should do. In a letter describing that meeting, she said that she begged him "to confirm on earth that which had been confirmed in heaven from all eternity." She added: "The confirmation of our course was what we did require" (Orchard 1985, 72; cf. Chambers II 1885, 135).

Pat Murray maintains that "as a leader Mary Ward was the first among equals." In support of this view she points to the well-known "Open Circle" picture that she sees as "an icon of leadership and authority in the Institute":

> For someone greatly inspired by Ignatius of Loyola and desiring to take the same way of life as the Society of Jesus, the circle speaks of a different type of organization, to that of the hierarchical structure conjured up by Ignatius' military model of religious life. The seating arrangement conveys a clear sense of equality, mutuality and respect among this group of women, but it is also clear that all eyes are turned towards Mary Ward who is seated at the edge of the Open Circle. (Murray 2005)

More than two hundred years later, Cornelia Connelly, founder of the Society of the Holy Child Jesus, was another strong leader who had to face much opposition. Like Mary Ward, she too adopted the Ignatian approach to discernment and leadership. Judith Lancaster makes an interesting comparison between two different accounts of her life and spirituality. She documents how the biography written by Bisgood during the period 1958 to 1961 "suggests that Cornelia's fundamental attitude to ecclesiastical authority was one of obedience; and the assumption in convent culture is that obedience is a certain road to finding the will of God" (Lancaster 2004, 168).

In sharp contrast to this, the account of Cornelia's life and virtues submitted in 1989 to the Sacred Congregation for the Causes of Saints has a rather different emphasis. It does not play down her very difficult relationships with various ecclesiastical authorities (Lancaster 203) and it acknowledges her independence of mind and force of character (p. 207). Lancaster's point is that the latter document not only represents a post-Vatican II outlook but was prepared by sisters and Jesuits who were enthusiastic about the new approaches in Ignatian studies (p. 215). For them, what was important was not blind obedience but personal and communal discernment.

Why?

All this raises the question of why, during the four hundred years prior to Vatican II, most of the religious congregations took on this very rigid style of leadership, while practically ignoring the discernment aspect of Ignatian thinking. The most obvious reason was that from the time of the philosopher Descartes in the seventeenth century—and even more so with the emergence in the eighteenth century of the movement called The Enlightenment—there was a great stress on being rational. This led to a serious questioning of the authority of the church. In reaction to this, the Vatican adopted a very authoritarian stance and condemned as a threat to church authority anything that seemed to put the emphasis on personal decision making.

Closely related to this was the fact that the Enlightenment valued thinking and rationality, over against feelings or religious experience. Even though the church leadership was quite hostile to much of what was represented by the Enlightenment, its theologians and leaders were nevertheless influenced by this current of thought. Consequently, they adopted an unduly rational, or rationalistic, style of thinking. There was a growing suspicion, especially in the Vatican, of spiritual feelings. This reached a high point a hundred years ago with the condemnation by Pope Pius X of Modernism. It involved rejection of what was thought to be an undue reliance on affectivity and the feelings of the heart. The condemnation of Modernism was seen as a defense against excessive subjectivity, which the Pope experienced as a threat to the objective authority of the church.

Furthermore, during the centuries between the Council of Trent and Vatican II, the church authorities generally identified with the ruling classes in European civil society, and modeled themselves on the highly authoritarian governments that they favored. This was despite the fact that on several occasions in different European countries the church found itself at odds with governments, and at times persecuted by them. Even in these situations it did not occur to the church authorities to identify with the poorer classes, the ordinary people.

In fact, at the time of the French revolution, and during the various subsequent revolutions and attempted revolutions over the following hundred years, the church leadership took the side of the conservative *ancien régime* and condemned the revolutionary movements in the strongest terms. It is not surprising, then, that leadership within the church itself became more and more authoritarian and centralized. It could even be argued that the Catholic Church, having adopted a mirror-image of the concept of the divine right of kings, applied it to the Pope and continued to hold on to it—and even to enlarge it—long after it had been abandoned in civil society.

Things might have been quite different. If the church leadership, in Rome and at the national level, had made a real option for the poor it is quite likely that this would have led to a quite different theology of authority. Since God is transcendent, divine authority is always mediated through human agents; and in principle there is no reason why these human agents should be the wealthy and the powerful.

Suppose the church authorities had come into real solidarity with the common people and taken the side of the poor against oppressive authorities. This would have had a feedback effect on the exercise of authority within the church itself. The church might then have developed a more democratic understanding of authority and a more collaborative approach to leadership. Instead of an insistence that rulers must be obeyed at all costs, the dominant idea would probably have been that the voice of the people is the voice of God (*vox populi vox Dei*).

Chapter 3

Authority and Leadership since Vatican II

The Second Vatican Council represented and legitimated a huge change in theology, in outlook and in spirituality on a whole range of issues. From the point of view of authority and leadership the two most important documents were the one on the church (*Lumen Gentium*) that said that the church is first of all the people of God, and the one on religious liberty (*Dignitatis humanae*) that emphasized freedom of conscience.

One could make a strong case for saying that, by and large, the religious congregations and missionary institutes took the full implications of these two documents far more seriously than the Vatican and the hierarchy did. In the years following the council, there was a dismantlement of authoritarian structures and attitudes in the great majority of the religious orders and missionary societies. In many cases there was, at first, little or nothing to replace the old spirituality of authority. So there was a period of experimentation that in some cases bordered on the chaotic. It sometimes happened that the main function of those who had been elected as superiors became largely that of taking the blame for individuals or groups who were largely doing their own thing.

However, this rather anarchical period did not last long. After a few years, there emerged in the various congregations and societies a new stress on a corporate searching for the original charism of the group. There was also a new emphasis on the sanctity of the individual conscience, balanced by a highlighting of responsibility to the group. Consequently, the old spirituality of blind obedience was largely abandoned and a new, more mature approach became the norm.

On the other hand, the way authority has been exercised in recent years by the Vatican and by many bishops has given rise to a serious crisis of authority in the Catholic Church. Much of the problem can be dated from 1968 when Paul VI issued *Humanae Vitae*, in which he rejected the view of the overwhelming majority of his advisory committee on the issue of contraception. This—and the subsequent way in which the issue has been handled—undermined the more-or-less implicit confidence most good Catholics previously had in the authority of the pope.

More recently the credibility of church authorities has been further weakened by the intransigent positions taken on the issue of the ordination of women and on a whole variety of issues such as the morality of homosexuality and masturbation, and the question of whether a husband who is carrying the HIV/AIDS virus may use condoms to avoid infecting his wife. Within the past ten years there has been a much more serious undermining of church authority due to the scandal of the sexual abuse of children by clergy and by the way in which that issue was handled by various bishops.

From Management to Leadership

This crisis of authority in the hierarchical church in the years and decades since Vatican II is not the whole story. During these same years there have been positive and interesting changes in the spirituality and practice of authority and leadership in most religious congregations and missionary institutes. Among them, various new developments took place—and some of the more recent ones are quite exciting.

One of the first changes was the taking over by religious groups of some of the structures and language of management in the secular world. In some cases the group who used to be called "The Superior General and his or her Council" came to be called "Central Administration." A little later some groups changed the title "superior general" to some variant of chief executive. At this time, too, religious groups began to employ management consultants to advise them how to organize their congregations or societies. The emphasis was on management.

It was only fairly recently that the emphasis shifted from management to leadership. Nowadays many religious congregations use the title congregational leader to describe the role that used to be played by the superior general or mother general. This shift is significant; I will spell this out in more detail when, in the next three chapters, I describe the new thinking about leadership in the secular world—especially in the fields of politics and of management.

Hand in hand with this new emphasis on leadership came three other important developments. One of these is the concept of team leadership. The second is the development of elaborate processes for consultation with the wider membership. The third is the new emphasis on models of communal discernment.

Most religious congregations and societies have adopted a system of team leadership. This means that, in practice, though not strictly in church law, the members of the council are no longer just advisers but really share responsibility for making and implementing policies and decisions. Furthermore, most leadership teams are deeply committed to a maximum degree of consultation and participation with the wider membership in the ongoing governance of the congregation. This model of team leadership and group participation is operative at every level, from the international right down to the local level.

The leadership teams of religious congregations frequently employ skilled facilitators to enable them to bond together as a team and to help them in their visioning and planning. They also employ facilitators to ensure that they get maximum participation from their members. Furthermore, many, if not most, of the leaders are themselves familiar with the use of facilitative skills. All this is in sharp contrast to the situation that prevails in much of the clerical and hierarchical side of the church. Here we still find a top down style of exercising authority. In general, the hierarchical side of the church has a very long way to go in the whole matter of developing a participative and collaborative style of leadership.

Contrasting Models of Authority

Why the difference between the way authority operates in the hierarchical-clerical side of the church and the way it is exercised in the religious congregations and missionary societies? The most obvious reason is simply the fact that leadership and authority roles in the congregations are elective offices that, in almost all cases, are occupied for a fixed number of years. After that period there is a further election in which those who hold the leadership role are either reelected or allowed to return to the ranks. This means that they are far less likely to become insensitive to the views of the regular membership than is a pope, a bishop, or even a parish priest—all of whom hold their office more or less permanently. If the elected leaders do go against the general will they are unlikely to be reelected.

The clerical culture is another serious obstacle to change to a more collaborative style. One element in this culture is a distrust of those who are not part of the in group. This means that the dominant views among the clergy can at times be in striking contrast to those of the laity. Furthermore, the clerical culture among diocesan clergy is often associated with a certain ambition to climb the ladder. Promotion is generally offered to safe men who are unlikely to rock the boat. And those who have attained positions of authority may be reluctant to relinquish or share their power and privilege.

A further reason why things have been so slow to change in the hierarchical church is that the movement toward team leadership has been pioneered mainly by women's congregations. Men seem to be more inclined to be hierarchical in their thinking and in their structures. The men's religious congregations have been slower in seeing the value of team leadership. However, following the example of the women's groups, most men's congregations have by now adopted team leadership in varying degrees.

The absence of women in the diocesan and hierarchical structures of the Catholic Church means that there has been little move toward participative and team leadership—and no encouragement from the top to do so. There have, of course, been some new church laws that stress the importance of parish councils and committees. But Rome itself has not set an example of collaborative ministry; by and large it has, in recent years, moved in the opposite direction. So this is one sphere where the religious congregations and societies have a prophetic role to play in the church.

There is one other reason why the religious congregations and missionary institutes have moved much further than the hierarchical church in developing a new practice and spirituality of authority and leadership. It is that, by and large, they are the ones who have taken the concept of option for the poor most seriously. As they have come more into solidarity with those who are victims of marginalization, discrimination, or oppression in society, they have become more aware of the dangers of the abuse of power. It is not surprising, then, that they have become more committed to implementing the new model and spirituality of authority and leadership in their own organizations. They have insisted on establishing structures, attitudes, and practices that allow for collaboration and participation of their membership in determining their institutes' policies and future directions.

It is worth adding that, in recent years, both the general membership and the leaders of religious congregations have at times had an experience of feeling powerless. They have felt themselves to be at the mercy of an oppressive use of authority exercised by the Vatican or by local bishops. For instance, there have been cases when the Vatican intervened to suspend the normal process of the election of a leader of a religious order. A much more common occurrence is where a bishop interferes unduly in the running of a hospital or school owned or staffed by religious sisters.

Religious communities that have had to put up with unwarranted interference from above are likely to be more sensitive to the ways power can be abused. From their own experience they have seen how some people who have a higher rank can be very aware of their higher status and can pull rank over others. They have also seen how many people who have higher rank tend to be unaware of the power and privileges that come with that rank and so can dominate others without realizing they are doing so (cf. Mindell 1995, 58). These religious communities are therefore more likely to adopt structures and models of leadership that have built-in safeguards.

Communal Discernment

One of the most important developments in recent years in religious institutes has been the making of a much clearer distinction between policy directions on the one hand and implementation of these policies on the other. It is now taken for granted in most congregations that every five or six years the general chapters of (mainly) elected delegates will lay down the key directions in which the congregation is to move in the next few years. This means that the primary task of those who are elected or appointed to leadership roles is to ensure that these policy directives are implemented. This is not to say that the authorities are reduced to being mere administrators. There is ample room—and need—for the exercise of leadership in guiding, facilitating, and inspiring the general membership to commit themselves effectively to the directions laid down at the chapter.

The Ignatian renewal of the past thirty years has seen the concept of communal discernment come to the fore. It has been of enormous benefit in enabling the membership of general and regional chapters or assemblies to establish their priorities and to take decisions on major policy issues. The shift from a parliamentary style of debate to a process of group discernment means that a deep spirituality pervades the decision making. The delegates to the chapters or assemblies are now consciously setting about looking for guidance from the Spirit in discerning the will of God. They are helped to do so by the employment of a process that integrates prayer into the decision making. Instead of engaging in arguments the participants are invited to share their spiritual feelings. When well carried out, this process encourages those who take part to avoid all rancor, special pleading, the riding of personal hobby horses, and backroom cabals. Ideally, it leads to convergence of views rather than polarization, and there is less chance that a small number of vocal people will dominate the discussion.

Over the years these various new developments have become grounded in the lived experience of many different groups. As this has happened, it has become evident that the new structures and techniques can go a long way toward making the exercise of leadership a rewarding—though quite demanding—experience for those who take it on. When taken seriously, the new approaches can also enable the general membership to have a real sense of involvement in setting the direction of the institute and in owning and implementing the major policy decisions that are taken. More importantly, they represent a very effective way of integrating spirituality with management and leadership.

Time and Maturity

On the other hand, experience shows that these new approaches put heavy time demands on all who take part in them. Those who take on a leadership role are committing themselves to what may sometimes be felt to be an endless series of meetings. So it is very important that they find ways to experience these meetings as life-giving rather than as energy-draining exercises that have to be endured and got through as quickly as possible. The same applies to the general membership if they wish to play an active collaborative and participative role in implementing the overall direction of the institute and in decision making at the local level.

Furthermore, it has become evident that the new approach to authority and leadership will work well only if the people adopting it are really mature. Personality weaknesses and immaturity show up quickly in planning meetings and in the way members carry out—or fail to carry out—the commitments they have taken on. This suggests that there is need for all who are involved to have a serious commitment to further training and a process of human growth; and many of them may require some measure of counseling or therapy. It is more or less essential that the leaders themselves should engage in a process of supervision of their work, to enable them to evaluate and improve the way they have been carrying out their leadership tasks—and to ensure that the pressures they experience do not lead to burnout.

Having looked at developments in relation to authority and leadership within the church over the centuries, I propose in the next three chapters to look at developments in civil society, first in the area of political thinking and then in the sphere of management theory.

Chapter 4

Political and Psychological Thinking

In ancient Greece, the city-state of Athens had a succession of different forms of government. One of these was a limited form of democracy—limited because the women and the underclass called helots did not have the right to vote in the assemblies. Reflecting on the political experiences of Athens and other Greeks city-states, the great philosophers Plato and Aristotle explored different forms of government.

Plato's Republic takes the form of a dialogue between Socrates and several others; it is generally taken that the views attributed to Socrates in the book are those of Plato himself. A key feature of Plato's Socrates is the analogy he draws between the different elements of the human person and the different classes in society. Just as the appetitive element must not be allowed to rule the human soul, so the irresponsible masses, ruled by their appetites, should not rule in the city-state. For Plato's Socrates, then, democracy should be replaced by aristocracy, that is, rule by the best—namely, the wise philosopher-kings.

Aristotle, in his *Politics,* was more even-handed. For him, the moral issue is not whether the city-state is ruled by one person, or by a small number, or by the many. It is whether the rulers govern well, that is, for the general good of the state; or whether on the other hand they rule badly, that is, to serve their own interests. Aristotle is against democracy if that means putting all the power in the hands of those who are poor. But he is equally against tyranny where all the power is in the hands of one person, and against oligarchy where all the power is in the hands of a few (bk. 3, ch. 7). What he wants to avoid is any system where power is exercised arbitrarily—whether that be by one ruler, or by a small group, or by the mass of the people. Instead, he wants a constitutional system where authority is attached to the office rather than to the individual who holds any particular office or position, and where the rule of law prevails (bk. 3, ch. 11).

From the time of the ancient Greeks up to about 1800 the democratic model of government remained out of favor in the political world. Most European countries had very authoritarian governmental structures—even those states that had gone some way toward elected government. Indeed, for much of this time, the theory of the divine right of kings was widely accepted. The French Revolution of 1789 overthrew the monarchy and attempted to introduce a measure of democracy. But within fifteen years, Napoleon had made himself emperor; he ruled France as an autocracy and dominated much of continental Europe.

In the 1780s, leaders of the newly independent United States gathered in a convention to debate the framework of the Constitution. The members "did not propose to set up an unlimited democracy . . . but they insisted on giving democracy its share in what they intended to be a balanced government" (Morison 1965, 309). When the issue came up about who would have the right to vote, they were not in favor of giving unrestricted voting rights to everybody. They could not agree about the extent to which suffrage should be restricted, so they left this matter to the separate states. In fact the franchise in most of the states remained quite restricted. In upstate New York, for instance, up to 1821, only farmers with a freehold of five hundred pounds a year were entitled to elect the Senators of the Upper House (Adler 2005). To protect the rights of property, it was considered necessary to restrict suffrage to the men of property. And, of course, women and slaves did not have a vote.

Meanwhile in Europe, after Napoleon was defeated, European leaders at the Congress of Vienna in 1815 tried to go back to older, monarchic structures of government. This attempt to turn back the clock had very mixed success. In the decades that followed there was a gradual movement toward a greater degree of democracy. However, it took the best part of another hundred years before universal suffrage became the norm in Britain and the U.S.A.

All through the nineteenth century the leadership of the Catholic Church—along with most of the other churches—remained quite hostile to democracy, insisting that power comes from God rather than from the people. It was only in the 1890s that Pope Leo XIII declared that democracy might be an acceptable form of government. And right up to Pope John XXIII's social encyclical *Mater et Magistra* in 1961, the Catholic Church remained radically opposed to socialism and even to any form of social democracy or welfare state.

The Leninist Approach to Leadership

Karl Marx, in his Communist Manifesto of 1848 and his other writings, envisaged a stage in which there would be a dictatorship of the proletariat (that is, the working class), as a first step toward a classless society. Lenin played a leading role in the Russian revolution and, having taken power, he attempted to put Marxism into practice in Russia. He developed Marxist theory along a particular line: for him, the masses could only come to revolutionary consciousness if they were manipulated and controlled by a tightly organized elite. This elite group would direct the discontent of the masses, channeling it in the direction that the elite considered to be the correct one. The task of the political elite group was to impose their party line on the masses.

It is quite surprising to find that many people in leadership roles today—either in government or in voluntary or church agencies—adopt this Leninist approach, even though they would totally disavow any similarity to Lenin. They imagine they and the small circle of their associates and friends know what is best for people; and they try to impose this or to manipulate people into following their line.

The most obvious example of this is the neo-conservative clique who exercise so much power in the U.S. government today—and one of whom, Paul Wolfowitz, was appointed head of the World Bank in 2005. This group see themselves as disciples of the German-born political philosopher Leo Strauss, whose followers are currently a major influence in the United States universities. In a recent book Anne Norton, a professor of political philosophy in Chicago, puts forward a convincing case to show that they are not at all in line with the older American conservative tradition (Norton 2004, 191). She maintains that they hold a profoundly aristocratic, antidemocratic view, namely, that "the ordinary people," or "the masses," or even "the uninitiated elite" cannot be trusted, because to do so would lead to chaos in society (Norton 98). So this particular elite group believe they must hold on to power and ensure that it is exercised in accordance with their convictions. In order to do so they have to manipulate "the ordinary people"—and so they ally themselves with evangelical and fundamentalist religious crusaders (Norton 178).

It might seem that all this has little relevance for people whose life is devoted to the church. But the well-known political philosopher Hannah Arendt suggests that ever since the time of Constantine the authorities of the Catholic Church have had an elitist understanding of the role of church leadership (Arendt 1977, 126–7). Certainly, there are grounds for saying that an elitist approach to the exercise of authority has been characteristic of an influential group in the Roman Curia since the early 1980s. They were alarmed at what they saw as the ever-increasing chaos in the church. They felt they knew best what is involved in living a Christian life today. This led them to discipline any theologians or local church leaders who, in their view, had stepped out of line.

Furthermore, these Vatican officials used the great credibility and popularity of Pope John Paul II to support and impose their views. They suggested that those who questioned these views were disloyal to the pope, to the church, and to the Catholic faith.

They sought to ensure that this same pattern would be followed also within each diocese. They also exerted considerable pressure on the various Catholic religious orders, congregations, and societies to keep their membership in line. In this latter project, however, they seem to have had a rather more limited success. The result is that at present a rather wide gap exists between the thinking and attitudes of the Roman Curia and the views of the great majority of the leaders of religious congregations.

Paulo Freire's Approach to Leadership

The elitist approach to authority and leadership is not accepted by all political philosophers. Several of those who were influenced by Marx rejected the Leninist idea that an elite group has to impose its party line. Of these, the most important from our point of view is Paulo Freire, the Brazilian educationalist who was born in 1921 and died in 1997. He had great success in literacy campaigns in Latin America and has inspired many who are engaged in training community leaders or social activists. A key feature of Freire's approach is that the leader must trust the people. For him, the key question the leader must ask is not: "How do I get people to follow me in taking the right action?" It is rather: "What is it that the people really want to happen, and how can I help them to achieve it?"

For Freire the place to start is with some "generative issue." By a generative issue Freire means a burning issue that will fire people up—one which generates in them real energy, such as excitement, eagerness, or anger. By focusing on such issues the leader will not have the task of trying to get people actively involved. It will rather be a question of tapping into and channeling the energy they already have around this issue.

Of course this raises the question of how to discover the most significant generative issues. The first point to note is that the generative issues will vary from one place to another and from one time to another. The second point is that the leader needs to involve a sizable number of the people concerned in a careful psychosocial analysis of the situation. So the group as a whole (or at least a significant number of them) is involved from the beginning in setting the agenda, and even in discovering what agenda needs to be set.

What is meant by a psychosocial analysis? It is a study of the situation that takes two aspects equally seriously. First, the *psycho* part means that one is trying to discover what issues people feel strongly about. For instance, they may be angry about one issue or excited about another, but in both cases there is plenty of energy in them, to get them motivated and moving. Second, the *social* part means that the group is looking at the social, political, and economic situation—and doing so in some depth, in a way that will reveal the root causes of the problems or issues about which people feel strongly. By locating these root causes the group has a much better chance of avoiding simplistic solutions. For instance, poor people in a particular area may be inclined to think that immigrants are taking their jobs; but by engaging in a search for the deeper causes of poverty they may be inspired to make common cause with immigrants in working for a more equitable and caring society.

Having identified some generative issues, the next step for those who follow the Freire methodology is the use of a participative technique that helps large numbers of people address these issues. Instead of just naming the issues for the people and urging them to action, the leaders use realistic dramas, pictures, simulation exercises, or other "codes" (as Freire called them) to explore the issues.

A crucial point for Freire is that in exploring these key issues, and in working out the action that needs to be taken, the leaders must not see themselves as the experts. Some of the leaders may have expertise or valuable experience in some aspects of the issue, but the people on the ground have an equally important contribution to make. So, all are teachers and all are learners. The effect of this approach is that, when changes are brought about, the people have a real sense of ownership of the process and its results. They know they have done the work themselves.

For those who wish to study Freire's ideas, the best place to start is probably his book *Education for Critical Consciousness* (Freire 1985). This book is much easier to read than his earlier and better-known book *Pedagogy of the Oppressed*. Those who wish to apply his ideas and approach on the ground in the training of community leaders and social activists can use the four volumes of the handbook *Training for Transformation: A Handbook for Community Workers* by Anne Hope and Sally Timmel (see Hope 1995 and 1999). Some years ago I published a book called *Integral Spirituality* the aim of which was to provide an expanded theological and spiritual background and foundation for the approach adopted in these training manuals. The book also includes further exercises and resource materials (see Dorr 1990).

Freire was thinking mainly of working with community groups for radical change in the wider society. However, his ideas can also be applied (with some minor modifications) to the exercise of leadership in an institution such as a hospital or school or in an empowerment program of any kind. His approach can also be adapted slightly and put into practice in the exercise of leadership within a religious congregation or missionary institute.

Arnold Mindell's Approach to Leadership

Having given a brief outline of Freire's approach to leadership, I want now to look at the work of a more recent thinker and innovator who has some fascinating ideas about leadership. Arnold Mindell comes from a New York Jewish background. He worked for some years in Zurich as a Jungian psychotherapist. Then he broadened his approach very considerably. From the point of view of leadership, the most significant of his innovations was his development of a process he calls "worldwork." This is a special type of workshop in which large groups of people tackle major sociopolitical issues such as racial prejudice, deep ethnic animosity arising from past or recent wars, gender issues, homophobia, and various other forms of prejudice.

Mindell's approach has a lot in common with that of Freire. One major point of similarity is that both Freire and Mindell emphasize the importance of strong feelings. Both are aware that the way effective change comes about is above all through the channeling of such strong emotions.

Because it takes the expression of feelings so seriously, Mindell's approach calls in question the usual rules (explicit or implicit) governing debate and dialogue. He encourages participants in his workshops to give expression to their strong feelings. This means that at times the atmosphere can get very heated and at other times people may be reduced to tears. The result is that the power in the group tends to shift from those who are good at thinking on their feet and expressing themselves clearly. The power moves more to those who feel passionately on certain issues and are willing to express these feelings in the group—even if they are not very good at putting them into nicely balanced words.

This also has important consequences in relation to how leaders (and others) can best manage conflict. First of all, they have to recognize that sometimes it is better not to try to put a lid on the expression of strong feelings. Second, they should accept that it is more helpful to think in terms, not of conflict resolution but of managing conflict—which may mean helping the group to live with the discomfort of divergent views. Third, in so far as there is a resolution of the conflict, it does not always come through the careful rational working out of a consensus position. Sometimes it is more likely to come through a kind of catharsis, that is, a release of high emotional tension in which people from opposite sides of the fence find themselves drawn together by a shared sympathy that enables them to accept each other in all their differences.

In Mindell's approach, leadership is exercised through a style of facilitation where one does not act as a judge or impartial observer who stands outside the process, avoiding emotional involvement in order to maintain neutrality and ensure that things do not get out of hand. On the contrary, the leader/facilitator is willing to become quite involved and moved. But the leader tries constantly to resonate with all the different viewpoints expressed. Above all, the aim of the leader will be to take the side of anybody who is being attacked or scapegoated. However, having successfully defended those who are being victimized, the leader does not have to stay on that side.

In the Mindell workshops the participants are encouraged to step deliberately into a role, that is, to take up a position where they speak with commitment on one side of an argument. The facilitator reminds the participants that they should distinguish between this role and the person who has temporarily taken on the role. Those who take on a role and speak strongly on behalf of that viewpoint, often find that they can then step back and be more open to listen to other points of view. As a result, they may find that they can authentically take up a different role a little later and speak on the other side of the argument.

When the distinction between the person and the role is understood and accepted, the participants begin to try out different roles. These roles give expression externally to the different voices that the participants hear within themselves and the different ways in which they find themselves pulled. This brings much greater flexibility into the dialogue. It often leads to convergence between those who had at first been strongly opposed to each other.

The facilitator who is following Mindell's approach sometimes names what is called a "ghost role." This phrase is used to refer to some figure or force that has been lurking in the back of people's minds and is influencing the group without being recognized or acknowledged. For instance, if members of the group have been engaging in a lot of blaming, the facilitator may suggest that there is a "judge" figure hovering invisibly over the group. This invisible judge is prompting the members to pass judgment on each other, or on themselves, or on some absent person or group. Once this ghost figure has been recognized and named the participants are able to deal with it and move on. As the participants become more familiar with the Mindell style, they no longer have to rely on the facilitator to notice and name these ghost figures; they can do it for themselves, and in this way become more involved in the facilitation of the process.

When dealing with leadership, Mindell introduces the concept of "eldership." What he has in mind is that there are various ways of being a leader. In addition to the usual active forms of facilitating, directing, inspiring, and persuading, there is also the quiet wise presence of "the elder." The style and contribution of the elder is so different from the more active styles of leadership that Mindell is unwilling to call the elder a leader, at least in the conventional sense of the term. He says: "The leader seeks a majority; the elder stands for everyone. The leader sees trouble and tries to stop it; the elder sees the troublemaker as a possible teacher. . . . The leader tries to act; the elder lets things be" (Mindell 1995, 184).

Mindell suggests that facilitators and leaders should make contact with the elder in themselves. They can do this by keeping an eye on the process going on within them, as well as recognizing the language and body signals of others in the group (p. 43). In this way they come in touch with the flow of energy in the group and are in a position to allow what needs to take place to happen. He maintains that they can do this through their awareness, without ever taking any outer action. "The leader needs a strategy; the elder studies the moment. The leader follows a plan; the elder honors the direction of a mysterious and unknown river" (p. 184). "Leaders know how to push for consent. The multicultural elder, however, is spiritual. By focusing on awareness, an elder makes something happen. Unexpected solutions appear at just the right moment" (p. 195).

One of the more important contributions of Mindell on issues of leadership is what he has to say about rank. He notes that there are many different spheres where an individual may have a higher or lower rank: some of the more obvious of these spheres are one's gender, one's race, one's degree of education, one's physical strength, one's wealth, one's job, one's psychological strength, and one's spiritual status. He points out that everybody has some form of rank. However, it is difficult for those who have higher rank in a particular situation to recognize that this gives them privileges and an advantage over others. On the other hand, those who have a lower rank are keenly aware of being at a disadvantage—and they become angry when they experience those with higher rank using their power without acknowledging what they are doing.

Those in any kind of leadership role should not aim to divest themselves of their rank but rather to be aware of that rank and to use it consciously and respectfully. An example of unawareness of rank is a remark said to have been made some time ago by a bishop speaking to a large group: "We are all equal here, from me down." Leaders should be keenly aware of the different kinds of rank possessed by various members of the group. The leader's aim should be to get these people to recognize their rank and use it with respect rather than using their higher rank to impose on others.

Mindell puts a lot of emphasis on "inner work." By this he means that the facilitators or leaders, while taking an active part in the group, and at times steering the dialogue in fruitful directions, are at the same time monitoring their own reactions. In this way they seek to ensure that they are not imposing their own views or biases on others. For Mindell, too, it is essential that the leader is able to "sit in the fire," maintaining balance and some degree of composure while strong feelings of anger or grief are swirling through the group—and perhaps through the leader's own consciousness as well. All this brings out the importance for anybody who takes on any kind of leadership role of engaging in personal counseling and of having supervision.

Like Freire, Mindell believes in the fundamental value of trusting the group rather than trying to impose on them an agenda or a particular line of thought or action. However, Mindell goes much further than Freire when he puts forward his very spiritual and challenging concept of "deep democracy." He argues that it is not enough to work for a consensus based on the majority view, even if it is a large majority. For him it is important to take particular account of the position of the out—or marginal people—in any community or organization. "Sustainable community—that is, deep democracy—dies if anyone's viewpoint, story or ideas are negated. . . . Deep democracy depends upon facilitating interactions between visionaries and 'non-believers'" (Mindell 1995, 176–7). This poses a serious challenge to the way most leaders work for consensus; it suggests that those in leadership should work much harder to listen to the dissident or awkward voices.

Chapter 5

The Limits of Democracy

In addition to Paulo Freire and Arnold Mindell, there is a third thinker who offers some stimulating ideas about the exercise of leadership and authority today. It is John Milbank, a British Anglican theologian well known in the field of social ethics. He is generally considered to be an author who adopts conservative positions in reaction against what he sees as unduly liberal views.

In a paper delivered to a conference in the Vatican in March 2005, Milbank put forward an impressive case against extreme liberalism, mainly in the sense of an understanding of human relationships in terms of gift. I focus here on just one significant point in his very comprehensive presentation. This is his claim that society needs to have a "monarchical" element and an "aristocratic" element as well as a democratic one (Milbank 2005, 3). The kernel of his argument is that those who opt for democracy alone are taking no account of objective truth or value. This leaves people at the mercy of the whim of the majority.

In putting forward his position, Milbank is not claiming to be entirely original. One can find echoes of his view in the thinking of the Founding Fathers of the American Constitution and, further back, in the works of Plato and Aristotle. But there is a welcome clarity in the way he expresses his position and there are many valuable elements in it.

Milbank is by no means rejecting the values of democracy. In fact he provides a solid theological foundation for the democratic concept of trusting the people. This foundation is that the people are potentially the *ecclesia* (the Christian community) and the Holy Spirit speaks through all: *vox populi, vox Dei,* the voice of the people is the voice of God (p. 3). However, he points out the dangers of what he calls "unqualified liberal democracy."

Milbank holds that the typical liberal democratic society tends to give too much power to the state. He rejects this. Instead he emphasizes the notion of subsidiarity, emphasized in Catholic social teaching. This involves respecting the integrity and values of local, regional, cultural, and religious communities or societies (p. 4). Furthermore, in line with Catholic tradition—and with the views Fritz Schumacher put forward in his famous book *Small is Beautiful*—he stresses the importance of small-scale local production (p. 6).

Mature?

In arguing that democracy has to be balanced by aristocratic and monarchical elements, Milbank points out that we are inclined to assume that society is composed of mature adults (p. 4). The reality, however, is that the young and the immature have to be educated and guided; it is only when they reach a certain maturity that they can play a full part in a democratic society. What this means in practice is that the role of parents in relation to their young or teenage children is more an aristocratic and monarchical role than a democratic one (pp. 4–5). Milbank seems also to assume that, even in adult society, some individuals are more fitted than others to play a monarchical or aristocratic role; and it would be difficult to disagree with him on this point.

What about a situation, such as that of a religious community, where one may assume that the vast majority are mature, responsible adults? Milbank would, I believe, claim that even in such circumstances there is need for a monarchical and aristocratic element alongside the democratic component. He maintains that in a genuine democracy there is an "irreducible moment of non-democratic decision which [the government] should be obliged to take responsibility for."

A government has to be trusted "to take its own decisions on the basis of justice and integrity, precisely because the electorate has previously endorsed its general principles, record and ethical character."

He argues that no appeal to opinion soundings and no "plebiscitory process of whatever kind can displace this 'monarchic' need for self-grounded decision taken 'under God.'" This, he says, is because "the people can never collectively be placed in the exact position that an executive power should occupy: of being (ideally) of the right human type, having enjoyed the right experience, receiving the right information, being able as an individual or small-group mind to arrive at a complex conclusion on the basis of complex reasoning" (p. 12).

Practical Applications

Milbank's position becomes fascinating and quite controversial when he applies his views to the situation in present-day Britain and America and makes concrete judgments. There is much validity in his criticism of abuses of democracy and extreme liberalism at the present time. But there seems to be a certain one-sidedness in his judgments. I think this arises because, understandably enough, his critique of current actual libertarian democracy is made in terms of a more ideal monarchical and aristocratic approach.

In order to balance this, we should note that in recent times we have also had many examples of abuse of monarchical power. Suppose Milbank's paper had been written in the early 1980s at the height of Margaret Thatcher's reign. At that time she was dismantling parts of the United Kingdom's social welfare system; and, during the Falklands/Malvinas war, she refused to take account of the United Nations once she had got its condemnation of the Argentinean invasion. Would it not then have been necessary to critique her monarchical approach? And, at the time I am writing this, it seems necessary to reject Tony Blair's monarchical approach on the issue of declaring war on Iraq. His stance is to be criticized as a failure to respect democratic values.

In relation to the United States, the issues are so obvious that I do not need to spell them out in any detail. Anne Norton puts forward a devastating case against the "neo-con" would-be elite group, who are abusing an "aristocratic" power (Norton 2004). Critics would say that the Bush administration has been misusing its monarchical powers in the kind of appointments it is making to such bodies as the United States Environmental Protection Agency, the World Bank, and the United Nations, and in manipulating public opinion in a way that allowed it to present the war in Iraq as part of the "war on terror." Another view could be that what they are abusing is their democratic power. But the fundamental point I am making is that we can find plenty of examples, both at the present time and in the past, of abuses not only of democratic power but also of aristocratic and monarchical power.

Milbank seems to overlook the fact that, alongside all the recent abuses of democracy and the present-day erosion of authentic politics, we can also find many instances where aristocratic and monarchical elements have been retained and even expanded in recent times. In the Constitution of the United States there is a deliberate separation of powers in which the judiciary is a check on the powers of the legislature and the executive. Most other democracies have a somewhat similar system, where the judiciary as an aristocratic power provides a balance to the more obviously democratic elements of the state. Quite recently the democratic governments of the United States and the United Kingdom have been taken to task by judges for abuses of the human rights of people accused or suspected of being sympathetic to "terrorism."

There are various other instances of beneficial restraint being imposed on the democratic component in government. One thinks of the introduction of ombudsman figures in various fields; and also of the increasing use in the United Kingdom and Ireland of aristocratic commissions (judicial or nonjudicial) to investigate and correct abuses. Where democracy has been abused in Ireland through clientism in relation to planning applications, power in local government has to be taken out of the hands of democratically elected councilors. The power is given instead to nonelected county managers, who exercise it in a more monarchical manner, or to a planning commission that exercises power in a more aristocratic way.

In the United Kingdom, the recent granting of independence to the Bank of England seems to be a positive move from a democratic to an aristocratic approach. The extent to which the democratic sovereignty of the United Kingdom parliament has diminished through the (reluctant) acceptance of rulings from Brussels, was a major move to temper democracy with aristocracy. This applies even more obviously to the acceptance by the United Kingdom and other European countries of rulings of the European Court of Human Rights and, more recently, of the jurisdiction of the International Criminal Court.

In the fundamental structures of the European Union the democratic powers of the European Parliament are limited by the aristocratic power of the Commission and the Council. Indeed, there were times when Jacques Delors, the president of the nonelected Commission, exercised a quasi-monarchical role in a beneficial way, for instance, by insisting on generous subsidies for the less-developed economies of Spain, Portugal, Greece, and Ireland. Even today the powers of the Commission are a means of ensuring that the democratic interests of the more populous countries (especially Germany) do not swamp those of smaller countries and entities.

Furthermore, on issues such as the preservation of fish stocks the Commission plays a key aristocratic role in restraining the short-term democratic/populist interests of fishermen (and their elected representatives) in Ireland, Portugal, Spain, etc. On issues of ecology, health, and safety the Commission's aristocratic powers provide a partial counterweight to the obvious ways in which the common market favors globalization and the swallowing up of local retailers by the giants, such as Tesco, Aldi, and Lidl. These various instances of aristocratic elements in modern-day society suggest that, while Milbank may be right in objecting to the excessive use of focus groups as a pandering to a misguided conception of democracy, his attack on "unqualified liberal democracy" is somewhat overstated. He is to some extent attacking a straw man, a model of government that does not actually exist.

However, at a more fundamental level, the examples of aristocratic elements I have cited can actually be used to support Milbank's basic argument that it is wrong to rely entirely on a rigidly democratic approach. For they indicate that, despite all the current rhetoric about the values of democracy, our present-day democracies rely to a considerable extent on aristocratic and monarchical elements.

There is, then, a strong case for agreeing with Milbank that we need aristocratic and monarchical dimensions to balance the democratic one. And this applies not merely to the constitution of states but also to organizations of all kinds. However, this leads on to a key issue: whom can we trust to exercise any of these roles? This issue is as old as Plato's Republic. We need wise rulers. But, as in the case of most other issues of practical ethics and politics, there is no general rule that provides the answer to the questions, "who is wise?" or "whom can we trust?"

There is no guarantee that a totally democratic system will result in good governance, either of a country or of an organization. A majority decision is not always a right decision; people can act for selfish motives or can be swayed by simplistic or deceptive arguments or persuasive individuals whose views are biased and mistaken. On the other hand, when a country or an organization is governed by an individual or a small group chosen because they are thought to be wise, this is no guarantee that serious mistakes and even abuses of power will not occur. These dangers can be lessened by the introduction of a legal system binding on everybody, together with constitutional safeguards such as a separation of powers between the legislative, the executive, and the judicial system. But no system can protect us fully against human folly and evil. We can, however, work out some guidelines which, if followed, will give us some assurance that authority and leadership will be exercised well. This is the issue I hope to address in chapters 7, 8, and 9.

The task I have set myself in this book is not to propose an ideal system of government for a country. What I am concerned with is an exploration of how authority and leadership can best be exercised in institutions and voluntary groups of all kinds, and particularly in religious organizations. Why then have I bothered to devote these two chapters to outlining a variety of political theories? It is because I believe that some very useful guidelines can be drawn from these theories. In chapters 7, 8, and 9, where I present my own views on leadership, I shall draw heavily on some of the key insights of the writers whose views I have outlined in these two chapters. However, before giving my own views about leadership, I shall devote the next chapter to a study of some of the new thinking in management theory, because here, too, we can find useful insights about the exercise of leadership.

Chapter 6

Leadership in Management Theory

In medieval times, business and craftwork were organized and controlled by merchant guilds and craft guilds. Authority in these guilds was exercised through an interesting mixture of familial and cooperative structures. Apprentices became effectively family members of the master, who trained them in their craft or profession and also played the role of a father—responsible not only for their work but also for their moral behavior. A primary purpose of the guilds was to ensure that their members had a monopoly in their particular segment of business or craftwork. And, like any monopoly, they could at times take advantage both of workers and of customers. However, at their best, the guilds ensured protection both for the producers and for the consumers.

The guild masters were generally more concerned with quality than with quantity. Apprentices were trained to take pride in their work. The result was that, generally speaking, the workers had a sense of personal involvement in their work. And they had a sense of ownership of the goods they produced. Ideally, at least, they were not just doing a job for the sake of the money.

With the industrial revolution in Europe in the nineteenth century there came a rapid development of capitalism. One of the effects was an increasing degree of specialization in work. The result was that workers found themselves just doing a job in order to earn enough to live on. They no longer had a sense of investing themselves personally in their work and had no sense of ownership of their product or of the enterprise. This is what Marx called the "alienation" of the worker. As the capitalist system has expanded more and more, this problem of the alienation of workers has become ever more serious. Within the past generation it has become a dominant feature not only in industry but also in the agricultural sphere, as smaller farmers go out of business and factory-farming and agribusiness become the norm.

From the point of view of the capitalist system the worker is a resource and an expense. The aim of the entrepreneur is to use all resources as efficiently as possible and to keep expenses as low as possible. In 1911 a management theorist called Frederick Taylor published a book called *The Principles of Management* that led to major changes in the way industry was organized. He proposed a "scientific" approach, based on the idea that specialization was the key to efficiency. According to "Taylorism" the task of managers is to standardize work by breaking up the production process into many distinct stages. At each of these stages there is a standardized task to be done, with standardized tools or machines. Workers are trained to specialize, each task being done in a standardized way by a particular group of workers who have been taught to do just this specific task. Management is organized in a hierarchical way, from the top down. Henry Ford carried this specialization approach a step further by introducing the assembly line in factories.

"Soft" Values

In more recent times management theorists have become aware that it is not sufficient to concentrate only on such hard values as efficiency in production and the bottom line (that is, profits). They have discovered that in the long run it is important also to pay attention to a variety of what are called "soft values." For instance, they realized that the work progresses more smoothly if there are good relationships between workers and management, and if the atmosphere in the workplace is one where workers feel respected and listened to (cf. Benefiel 2005, 24, 66). Other soft values are a sense of involvement and fulfillment by employees in the particular work they are doing and in the enterprise as a whole, as well as the promotion of creativity among the workforce. A further soft value is the fostering of good relationships between the enterprise as a whole and the local community. Management consultants also came to appreciate how important it is for any enterprise to develop a reputation for honesty in relation to its customers and potential customers, and a good record for reliability in servicing the product and in follow-up.

There were different reasons why these soft values came to be appreciated. Some managers and entrepreneurs felt it was wrong to treat workers as soulless automatons by making them do work in which they had no sense of ownership and pride. Some came to realize with shock that the managers themselves were being damaged by having to treat workers not as persons but purely in terms of their productivity; and by being part of a system that put a premium on competition rather than cooperation and respect. So they wanted to foster the soft values for moral reasons.

This moral concern was not really new. A small number of firms had, at various times, pioneered an alternative more humane and respectful approach. Some industrial and agricultural enterprises are organized on cooperative lines, where the workers are the owners. One outstanding example is the Mondragon cooperative project in Northern Spain that currently employs about 55,000 workers. Other examples of a more humane and moral model of work are some enterprises owned by Quakers (members of the Society of Friends). However, all these were very much the exception, and they have had little impact on mainstream capitalist society.

The really new element in management theory in more recent times was the realization that soft values are worthwhile, not merely from a moral point of view but even from a narrowly economic point of view. Management consultants and theorists came to realize that soft values can actually increase productivity because workers who are not at peace with themselves and others will not work well (cf. Benefiel 2005, 35). Any enterprise that seeks to flourish over a long time span needs to take on board the soft values noted above and in the next paragraph. This realization is bringing about a significant shift in the approach of most major firms. At the cutting edge of this process are those business leaders who have consciously set out to introduce—or reintroduce—spirituality into the workplace. This in turn has led many writers to produce a large and ever-growing literature that sets out to describe and promote this movement. Among the more recent studies are Margaret Benefiel's *Soul at Work* (2005) and Sue Howard and David Welbourn's *The Spirit at Work Phenomenon* (2004).

The soft values can be categorized into five different types. First, there are those that have to do with a person's desire to achieve personal authenticity, including intellectual and emotional honesty and even transparency. Second, there are values associated with promoting better human relationships within the workplace and with the local community. Third, there are the values concerned with stimulating management and workers to greater creativity. Fourth, there are such moral values as respect for the environment and protection of the poor people who harvest primary products such as coffee or tea. Finally, there are more overtly spiritual values, such as a sense of inner peace and serenity, as well as a sense of meaning in life in general and a sense of personal purpose or vocation. At their highest, these spiritual values are quasi-mystical values. For many people they involve having a personal relationship with God. But there are many others who associate them with a sense of harmony and oneness with nature or with some nonpersonal Absolute.

In the preceding paragraph I have given a rather simple listing of different spiritual values. Those who would like a more sophisticated and detailed account of various stages of personal and corporate growth in spirituality can find such an account in Richard Barrett's book *Liberating the Corporate Soul* (1998); and there is a useful summary of Barrett's position in Howard and Welbourn's *The Spirit at Work Phenomenon* (2004, 164–5).

Teams and Coaching

As a result of the new awareness of the importance of good relationships in the workplace there has been a very serious questioning of the "Taylorist" approach. Nowadays many factories and other enterprises no longer go for narrow specialization. Instead, the employees are organized into work teams. Operating in a team gives the workers a much greater sense of ownership of the work they are doing; and it encourages creativity in the workers.

The teams usually include one or more of the management people. Within the team these managers do not flaunt their higher rank. They are on first-name terms with the other team members. And—ideally at least—they are prepared to listen to suggestions from the other team members about better ways of doing the job and coping with difficulties. It has been shown that this team approach can generate a much better relationship between workers and managers. There is less absenteeism and workers are more likely to stay on with the company because they find the atmosphere congenial and supportive (see Bowman 2004).

Many of the larger companies have gone a step further. They provide a "coaching" service for their employees—first of all for those in management roles but also, to a more limited extent, for the regular workers. The work coach is really a counselor who is available to help an employee experiencing difficulty in coping with the work situation. Quite frequently, in fact, no strict line of division is made between the work situation and the other aspects of the employee's life.

Promoting Creativity

In recent years there has also been a great emphasis in management theory on the importance of promoting creativity. There is a new awareness that workers at every level are not only more fulfilled and content but also more productive when they are encouraged to find creative ways of carrying out their work.

Nowadays, workshops on creativity in the workplace are being organized both by university departments of management and by more overtly spiritual agencies such as the Findhorn Foundation, a spiritual center located in Northern Scotland.

One of the best-known management consultants in the world is Edward de Bono. In his website he claims to be the inventor of the concept of "lateral thinking." This means thinking in a more imaginative way, rather than in the conventional logical step-by-step manner. Lateral thinking helps us to question the assumptions we had previously taken for granted (see de Bono 1990).

Perhaps the most valuable tool invented by de Bono to promote creativity is his "Six Thinking Hats" process (see de Bono 2004; and www.edwarddebono.com/). The basic insight behind this process is the realization that we can deal with a problem or challenge much more effectively if we look at it from a variety of different points of view. Here I shall give only a brief outline of what it involves since it is best learned through a practical workshop.

De Bono noticed that when a group of people are deliberating about whether or not to take a particular course of action, different people in the group approach it from different angles. The optimists focus mainly on the advantages of the proposed action, the pessimists put up various objections, the practical logical people focus on the facts of the case, those who are influenced mainly by their feelings or hunches take sides on the basis of their sense of what should be done, while the more imaginative people come up with various creative alternatives.

Realizing the value of all of these different approaches, de Bono proposed that instead of leaving each of these different roles (optimist, pessimist, creative person, etc.) to just one or two members of the group, all the members should deliberately take on each of the roles in turn. His process provides a way of doing this, through the use of different colored hats. By wearing a particular color hat the members of the group remind themselves of which role they are taking on at any particular stage of the process.

When focusing objectively on the relevant facts or data of the situation, they all wear white hats. When thinking and speaking optimistically of the benefits and advantages of the proposed course of action, they all put on yellow hats. When they come to focus on the disadvantages and the reasons for not taking the action, they all put on black hats. When sharing their feelings and hunches about what should or should not be done, they all wear red hats. When setting out to think laterally, outside the box in an imaginative creative way, and coming up with alternatives and new ideas on the subject, they put on green hats.

Finally, de Bono suggested that there is need for one or more members of the group to think about how best to organize the whole process. This managing role is symbolized by the wearing of a blue hat. Whoever wears the blue hat focuses on defining the problem, suggesting which of the other hats should be used at different stages, monitoring the correct use of the different hats, and eventually summing up and spelling out the conclusions that have emerged.

Planning groups who adopt this approach find it a useful and creative tool. It has the effect of bringing to the discussion far more information and more creative options than would otherwise have emerged. It also ensures that both the advantages and the difficulties associated with the proposed course of action are explored quite thoroughly. In general, it acts as a stimulus to the group to address all their issues in a creative way rather than focusing on just one or two aspects of the question, or getting bogged down in arguments. Furthermore, it reminds each of the members that they can be more flexible in the way they address an issue, rather than allowing themselves to be limited to adopting a particular attitude and stereotyped into playing a particular role in the group.

We may note in passing one key similarity between the approach of de Bono and the Ignatian communal discernment process: each of them invites the participants in the discussion to avoid taking one side or the other at the beginning of the discussion. The participants are asked to suspend their judgment while all of them look together at the advantages of the proposed course and action and, separately, at its disadvantages. This helps to avoid polarization and one-sidedness.

Moral and Spiritual Values

In recent years there has been an increasing emphasis on moral and spiritual values in business. Some of this new emphasis is coming from reflective and socially conscious management theorists. But most of it comes from two other sources. On one side there is pressure from social activists who can threaten to organize a boycott of a company that does not respect key environmental or social values. On the other side are some exceptionally wealthy business people who take account of these values either because it will give their businesses a good image, or because they themselves are committed to these values and are prepared to put their money where their mouth is. Anita Roddick, who founded "The Body Shop," pioneered this new approach (cf. Howard and Welbourn 2004, 150). Currently, over half of Europe's largest companies carry out what are called "environmental audits" to ensure that they take account of environmental values; and a number of the big companies also carry out "social audits" (Hertz 2001, 127–8).

It is not unusual now to find management consultants insisting on the value of spirituality in the workplace. Quite frequently they distinguish sharply between spirituality and religion, favoring the former but not the latter, mainly on the grounds that religion may be divisive. When they refer to spirituality they generally have in mind such values as, harmony, trust, good communication, cooperation, transparency, and honesty.

One of the more interesting processes designed to promote spirituality in the business world is a workshop entitled "Frameworks for Change." This was designed by two women, Joy Drake and Kathy Tyler. While living in the Findhorn Foundation in Scotland they created "The Transformation Game," a widely used process that helps people develop their personal spirituality and their intuitive capacities. "Frameworks for Change" is a major adaptation of "The Transformation Game."

The "Frameworks" workshop is tailored specifically for the members of management teams. For this reason it employs a more secular language that is close to the idiom used by management consultants in the world of business. It focuses primarily, not on personal spiritual development, but on values immediately relevant in the workplace and especially among working teams. The Frameworks process is very effective in helping participants develop such "soft values" as creativity, empathy, respect for teammates, and personal integrity.

In its later stages the Frameworks process invites the participants to go beyond issues of personal serenity and good relationships in the workplace; it offers them the opportunity to look at the overall purpose of the institute in which they are working and to situate the institution and themselves in the context of such global issues as racism, sexism, ecological degradation, and social injustice. In this way it helps the participants avoid an unduly narrow conception of spirituality that has become fairly widespread in recent years. It invites them to integrate into their spirituality a practical ethical concern that is quite universal in scope. (For a fuller account see Dorr 2002, 206–13.)

Though this workshop was originally designed for use in the business world, I have used it extensively with the leadership teams of religious organizations and occasionally with those in management in nongovernmental agencies. They have found it particularly useful in helping them to integrate their spirituality with their practical issues of management and leadership. I have also used a scaled-down version of the process, called "The Frameworks Coaching Process," that the creators of the workshop have made available more recently. (For further information about these two processes see www.innerlinks. com/frameworks.)

Tim Bowman's Research

There is a very practical illustration of much of what I have been saying about "soft values" in some recent research conducted by Tim Bowman, an engineer who worked for twenty-two years in a research and engineering center of the Ford Motor Company in Britain. While he was working there as an engineer/business analyst he undertook a major study of the management policies and practice in the Ford Motor company on a worldwide basis, with special reference to its center at Dunton in Essex where the number of workers is around 5,000 (Bowman 2004, 181).

As an insider, Bowman had a head start in finding the right kind of questions to ask in his interviews and questionnaires. As an employee who was well known and already had good relationships with many of the employees, he was trusted by both managers and regular workers. So he was able to get information and views that people might otherwise be reluctant to give. Furthermore, he had access to the results of an enormous number of evaluation questionnaires that the company had asked workers to respond to, quite independently of Bowman's own research.

In his recent doctoral dissertation (which he has generously allowed me to draw on and quote), Bowman presents the results of his exhaustive research. What emerges from his study is that the people in top management positions in Ford advocate or aspire to the soft values approach; and these values are being embodied in the official management policies of the company (pp. 109–78, 276). Furthermore, his research shows that in Ford the employees also have a very strong desire that these soft values should permeate the workplace (e.g., pp. 239–40, 254–7).

Bowman's research shows that many of these soft values are actually implemented in at least one experimental unit in the company and specifically in situations where teamwork is the norm. For the most part, however, the old style of top-down and authoritarian management is still in operation. The problem is that those in middle management, as well as at least some of those in upper management, were chosen and trained according to the old criteria; and these managers have not changed their attitudes and approach.

In recent years, Ford has invited their management people to use the Myers-Briggs Type Indicator (MBTI) that enables people to be classified in relation to different facets of their personality and style. When Bowman examined the results, he discovered something quite significant. He found that an unusually large proportion (86 percent) of the present middle managers are people who rate highly on "T" (thinking) and low on "F" (feeling). Bowman's conclusion is that the vast majority of these managers will tend "to lead through impersonal logic, reasoning and analysis, and as necessary coercion. Only an insignificant minority will tend to lead through personal charisma and relationships, and to emphasize values" (p. 266). Bowman recognizes that personality types represent innate preferences and should not be taken in a deterministic sense. Nevertheless he notes that the employees "are keenly aware of the incompatibility between the styles of prevailing management . . . [and] . . . the future visions and ideals pronounced by the corporation" (p. 266).

In the light of Bowman's research it is possible to suggest some tentative conclusions even though these are not explicitly stated by Bowman himself. It is possible that intense and ongoing retraining would enable some of the existing management people to learn to go against their innate inclination and adopt a more congenial style. But it would seem that if Ford really wanted to carry through on their commitment to adopt soft values, they would have to sideline or get rid of many of the present management and choose and train up a whole new contingent. These would be people of a quite different type of personality with a notably different way of relating to the workers—and to each other. Bowman himself puts forward a case for having managers elected by the workforce rather than appointed as at present; and he argues that this is by no means an unrealistic idea (pp. 277–8). His central theme, however, is the need for a change in the type of authority exercised by managers. He believes that the appropriate behavior style is one he would characterize as the "servant" type.

There is an important lesson in this for those who are interested in changing the way leadership is exercised in the church or in church-related organizations or voluntary agencies. The lesson is that it is not enough to adopt new official policies that give preference to respect for the person and improving human relationships over an authoritarian or bureaucratic style. It is also necessary to choose leaders who are temperamentally in tune with these new policies—and to offer them the kind of training that will enable them to develop their gift for putting this new model of leadership into practice.

This is not to say that there is little or no place in leadership for those whose personality shows an innate preference for the thinking function rather than the feeling function. One of the great advantages of team leadership is that the team can be composed of members of different personality types. Each of the team members can then contribute the particular gifts characteristic of that type of character, and together they can form a balanced team.

The Covey Approach

There is one other management consultant and author whose views I would like to outline before going on in the next chapters to present my own thoughts on the nature and exercise of leadership. This author is a professor of business studies called Stephen Covey who, about twenty-five years ago, wrote a book called *The Seven Habits of Highly Effective People*. That book sold millions of copies in many languages and became a kind of bible for those in management positions. Covey became a management consultant to many of the world's largest and most prestigious companies, and subsequently to the governments of several countries.

In 2004 Covey published a new book called *The 8th Habit: From Effectiveness to Greatness*. In his new book he shifted his main focus from management to leadership. His account of what is involved in leadership gives a high priority to spiritual values. He succeeds in integrating the spiritual element into his overall vision of leadership.

From one point of view the most important aspect of the book is not what is being said but who is saying it. Coming from this widely celebrated management guru, the spiritual message carries great credibility. But I must add at once that, quite apart from the fame of the author, the book contains some exceptionally helpful material on leadership.

Finding One's Own Voice

A preliminary key point made by Covey is that management is of things, whereas leadership is of people. In this age of knowledge, people cannot be managed as though they were things. Covey maintains that one needs to use a "whole-person paradigm" in becoming a leader. This means taking account of what Covey sees as the four key aspects of the human person, namely, the mind, the body, the feelings, and the spirit (Covey 2004, 20–4).

For Covey there are two stages in leadership. The first is finding one's own voice—knowing what one stands for and being able to take a firm, clear stance on key issues. He maintains that it is only when this has been accomplished that one can go on to the second stage of leadership, which is inspiring and helping others to find their voices. He applies his "whole-person paradigm" to both stages of leadership.

He looks first at the question of finding one's own voice as a leader, and takes each of the four dimensions of the human person in turn:

- To find one's own voice one must meet the need of the mind to have vision. For Covey, vision includes creativity, idealistic dreaming, thinking strategically, and reflection.

- Next, one must also ensure that the body has discipline. He sees discipline as giving one the ability to take action and to be consistent and tenacious in continuing under pressure.

- Third, in order to find one's own voice as a leader, one must ensure that there is real passion at the feeling level. For Covey, this involves strong commitment and it includes hopefulness and courage.

- Finally, one must take seriously the need of the human spirit to act according to conscience. This means taking one's responsibility seriously and being wise, respectful, and compassionate (Covey 2004, 67). He says:

> Vision is seeing with the mind's eye what is possible in people, in projects, in causes and in enterprises. . . . Discipline is paying the price to bring that vision into reality. It's dealing with the hard, pragmatic, brutal facts of reality and doing what it takes to make things happen. Discipline arises when vision joins with commitment. . . . Passion is the fire, the desire, the strength of conviction and the drive that sustains the discipline to achieve the vision. . . . Conscience is the inward moral sense of what is right and what is wrong. . . . It is the guiding force to vision, discipline and passion. (pp. 65–6)

Inspiring Others

In the later part of the book Covey moves on to the second aspect of leadership, namely, inspiring others to find their voice. He begins this part by saying: "Leadership is communicating to people their worth and potential so clearly that they come to see it in themselves" (p. 98). This indicates that he sees leadership primarily in terms of empowerment of people rather than trying to control or manage them.

It is interesting to see what happens when Covey applies his "whole-person paradigm" at this second stage. In the vision area what is now needed is not just a personal vision but a common vision. So the leader should not start off by trying to impose his or her own vision on others. Instead, the leader needs to set up a process in which people are invited to share their vision and values with him or her and with each other. This is what Covey calls "pathfinding."

Corresponding to discipline of the body at the first-stage (personal) level, what is needed at the second stage is an effective system. This system is one that will ensure that the organization and the people in it implement the common vision, and focus most energy on "what matters most." Covey calls this "aligning" because it involves establishing a system appropriate for, or aligned with, the purpose of the organization. This is where the good management aspect of leadership comes in.

Next he moves to the sphere of feelings in the context of enabling others to find their voice. Corresponding to passion at the personal stage, what is required at this second stage is empowerment of people. The aim here is to evoke in the group a wholehearted commitment and dedication to the purpose of the organization. The way in which the leader does this is by helping them to recognize their own talents and gifts. People's feelings become engaged and they are likely to devote themselves heart and mind to the project when they are working under the guidance and inspiration of a leader who values them and helps them discover their giftedness.

Finally Covey looks at the sphere of the human spirit. In this area, as we saw, leaders who wish to find their own voice must follow their conscience. When leaders set out to help others find their voice, what is required of them is what Covey calls "modeling." He holds that this is the central aspect of leadership. As he describes it, it is the point where finding one's own voice comes together with helping others find their voice.

Covey says: "it is only when people actually experience for themselves how a conscience-driven person models pathfinding, aligning and empowering that leadership actually takes place" (p. 127). What this means in practice is that the leader—together with colleagues in a leadership team—acts morally and respectfully in implementing the other three aspects of leadership of an organization. These are: working to create a common vision (pathfinding), the setting up of an effective system (aligning), and the empowering of people.

The crucial point is that it becomes evident from the manner in which the leader carries out these tasks that the leader is conscience-driven. This attitude then begins to percolate through the whole organization. Those who are working there pick it up, practice it, and feel supported in doing so. The leader has modeled a style others are happy to follow and make their own.

Covey remarks that in some cases the inspiration of the leader may be so powerful that people are willing to adopt the leader's vision even if they have not been involved in shaping that vision (p. 127). One thinks here of Gandhi, Mandela, Aung San Suu Kyi, and, of course, of the great religious leaders like Jesus, Muhammed, and Buddha.

There are several virtues that Covey holds are important in modeling. Among them are being personally trustworthy and trusting others, listening very carefully and respectfully to the views of others, being humble, being willing to apologize when one has made a mistake or has done wrong. He maintains that leaders should think in terms of abundance rather than of competition. That means they should assume there are plenty of good things to go around, so they can avoid the mistake of imagining that if others in the organization gain some benefit, it must be at the expense of the leader. Closely related to this is Covey's insistence on the importance of always looking for a "win-win" outcome of any disagreement—that is, finding a way in which neither side feels they have lost the argument (pp. 149–50, 167–76).

All in all, Covey's approach is both practical and inspiring. Those who are called to exercise any kind of spiritual leadership will find in his book much that is valuable.

Chapter 7

Four Kinds of Leaders

In the following three chapters, my intention is to present my own ideas on the exercise of authority and leadership. In doing so, I shall draw freely on the insights of the saints, philosophers, and management consultants whose views and approaches I have outlined in previous chapters.

What is Leadership?

The word leadership is ambiguous. It can refer to the person or persons in charge of or in command of a country, a community, an organization or any other group; for instance, we can speak of the government of a country or of an organization as the leadership. But leadership is also used to refer not to the person or persons who are the leaders but to the activity or ability of this person or these persons; for instance we speak of a person giving leadership, or of somebody having leadership qualities, meaning the ability to exercise leadership well. In this book—and particularly in the present and the next two chapters—I am taking the word in this latter sense.

Leadership in this more active sense is such a complex reality that it is difficult to define it comprehensively. I offer the following practical working description. Leadership is the influencing, motivating, guiding, directing, or coordinating of individuals, groups, communities, or organizations in a way that affects their behavior or actions, especially in relation to bringing about change or resisting change.

What is required if authority and leadership are to be exercised well? First of all, there is need for some gifted individuals who, understanding what leadership involves, are willing either to put themselves forward as possible leaders or at least willing to accept a leadership role if they are asked by the group, or by those in a higher level of leadership, to take on this task.

A second need must also be met if leadership is to be successful. It is the need for an appropriate framework within which authority and leadership are exercised. This framework will be laid down partly in constitutions and laws, and partly in traditions and established practices.

Third, the possibility of good leadership is also affected by the views and attitude of the people to whom the leader is asked to provide leadership. It is important that they have some degree of shared understanding with the leader about the nature of authority and leadership. We might call this a philosophy of leadership, provided we realize that it will include sociological and psychological elements. For the religious believer, this philosophy will be taken up into a theology and spirituality of leadership.

If leadership is to be exercised in a truly moral way, a fundamental part of the shared philosophy and spirituality of leadership should, I believe, be a general acceptance that the members of the group have both a right and a duty to be actively involved in establishing and reviewing the overall direction in which the community wishes to move. Another part should be a willingness of the group and its present leaders to be on the lookout for people who have the talents and the virtues that make them capable of providing that kind of participatory leadership.

The leader who is a committed Christian will add a further vital element, namely, awareness of the central role of the Holy Spirit. There is one major point of agreement between the different traditions of spirituality I looked at in the early chapters of this book. It is that the starting point of a Christian understanding of authority and leadership should be a commitment to being led by the Spirit.

The Lone Leader

I propose now to describe four types of leader, while recognizing there may be a considerable overlap between the different types. The first type of leader is the person who, like St. Francis of Assisi or Buddha, has a very personal vision and sets out to follow it with little or no intention of trying to lead others. However, many others are in fact inspired by the single-minded integrity with which this person answers his or her personal call, and so they gather around and become followers of this person.

Leaders of this kind see their primary focus as being personally authentic in following their star. They may feel that they could be distracted from their vision and their call, and their integrity and their purpose could be undermined or contaminated, if they set about attracting or inspiring others. To do so, they may feel, could introduce a certain element of calculation and compromise. It might even lead them to try to curry people's favor by putting on some kind of act.

They may eventually come to accept that their lives and actions do in fact inspire others, and that others want to follow them. But for them this is a kind of byproduct of the stance they have taken, rather than something at which they have aimed directly. For that reason it may be appropriate to call this type of person the *lone leader*.

This kind of leader is quite likely to relish the truth of a cryptic phrase in the Hindu Scripture called the Bhagavad Gita. One of the characters there is told to "relinquish the fruits of action." This suggests that any action should be undertaken because it is intrinsically worthwhile rather than for some utilitarian purpose like influencing others or trying to impress people.

It is helpful here to recall Covey's approach. He holds that the first stage in leadership is finding one's own voice. Leaders need to know what they believe in. They need to have some personal vision and purpose—and the discipline and passion to stand up for the truths and values that give meaning to their lives. As we shall see later, it is largely by modeling this vision and commitment that leaders inspire others.

The Emergent Leader

While it is true that every leader needs to have a personal vision that is to be followed with integrity, most leaders do not see it as a distraction from their purpose to be concerned about sharing their vision with others and inspiring them to follow the same call. In fact, the type of lone leader I have just described is quite rare. Much more common is a second type I would call the *emergent leader*. What I have in mind is a situation where a group of people have been coming together, gradually working out a shared vision. Over a period of time it becomes evident that one or two of the members of the group have particular leadership gifts. They are good at enabling the group to reach consensus and at articulating the common vision. They may also have a gift for nurturing good relationships within the group, at resolving tensions, at keeping the energy of the group high—mainly through finding ways to keep everybody "on board" and actively involved.

The members of the group come to value these leadership gifts; and the emergent leader also recognizes that he or she is playing a leadership role, and becomes willing to take on this role more consciously. So, ideally, this person becomes a spokesperson and representative of the group, acting on their behalf and with their full support. After some time this emergent leader may be formally appointed by the group to an official leadership role. But, even if this does not happen, there is no doubt that the person is exercising real leadership both within the group itself and in its relationship with the outer world.

I have described these two types of leader separately, but in practice one frequently shades into the other. The emergent leader may have started off with a very personal vision but gradually discovered that this vision is shared in some degree by others. So this person comes together with like-minded people both to articulate their shared vision and to try to implement this vision in the real world. It is within this common project that the leadership potential of the person comes to be recognized and given full scope. Many instances of this kind of leadership can be found in women's groups and in groups working on such issues as ecology or justice.

The Classic Leader

There is a third type of leader: somebody who has a very personal vision, but one that cannot be realized without the involvement of many others. An obvious example is Gandhi whose vision was of a free India attained through a nonviolent struggle. One might also think of Aung San Suu Kyi and her vision of freeing her country of military dictatorship. Leaders of this type are quite the opposite of the first type because, almost from the start, their aim is to inspire others to share their vision.

We are dealing here with what we may call the *classic leader*— one who has a burning personal vision and at the same time has found ways of inspiring hundreds or thousands or even millions of others to adopt that vision and follow the leader in working and struggling to implement it. How does this inspiring of others take place? It generally involves an ability to relate well to others, in some cases in terms of warmth and near intimacy and in other cases through the projection of a powerful, almost dominating personality. Frequently, too, it is done through a mixture of rousing speeches, stimulating and convincing writing, and carefully chosen actions such as rallies, protest meetings, and marches. What is particularly important is the engagement by the leader in key symbolic actions, such as Gandhi's salt march or his burning of British cotton. These symbolic actions touch into what Paulo Freire calls the generative issues of the people whom the leader wishes to inspire.

Some people have the talent to be leaders of this kind while others do not. What makes the difference? It seems to be a particular charisma that is difficult to pin down. Fundamentally it involves a certain projection of energy, through which the leader draws others into the leader's own vision and conviction. And this vision is one of transformation, of a world that will be different and that already seems different when experienced through the eyes of the leader. This coming together of the present reality with the vision of a transformed future is well expressed in the well-known (even hackneyed) lines from a poem by Wallace Stevens:

> They said, 'You have a blue guitar,
> You do not play things as they are.'
> The man replied, 'Things as they are
> Are changed upon the blue guitar.'
> And they said then, 'But play, you must,
> A tune beyond us, yet ourselves,
> A tune upon the blue guitar
> Of things exactly as they are.'

I have suggested that it is helpful to think in terms of a projection of energy when we try to understand this ability of the leader to communicate his or her vision to others. One of the advantages of interpreting it in this way is that we can see that after some time the energy begins to flow in both directions. Leaders of this kind not only share their own energy but also draw on the energy of the group—more especially when the group is gathered together, but also, less obviously, when the members of the group are dispersed.

We may think, for instance, of how Nelson Mandela, while still in prison, became a focal point for the resistance of millions of people to the apartheid system. In such situations the leader becomes the focus for what may at first be a rather scattered group energy. This diffuse energy is taken in and then projected back out to the others in a more concentrated form—directed toward the realization of the vision of the leader. By sharing his or her own faith, the leader is generating a similar faith in others; and the leader is in turn being nourished by their faith. This creates an upward spiral of energy.

A little reflection on real-life situations suggests that, while a central part of leadership is this ability to stir up people by sharing a vision, this is not sufficient. The leader must also have some further gifts. The first of these has to do with taking risks and making decisions. The person who gets paralyzed when confronted with practical choices is very unlikely to be an effective leader. Leaders need to be decisive, to be willing to take the risk of opting for a particular course of action, while knowing that it may emerge later that a different choice would have been better.

At the same time the leader must not be impetuous, unable to wait for the opportune moment. The decision to bide one's time is itself a decision; it is by no means a failure to decide. So the leader needs to have good judgment. This involves an interesting mixture of deliberation and intuition. Deliberation is the more rational aspect, a weighing up of the available information and of the foreseen consequences of possible courses of action. However, life is so unpredictable that anybody who wants to rely entirely on a rational calculation of possible outcomes is likely to become indecisive and almost paralyzed when faced with difficult choices. So leaders have to rely also on their intuition. This gives a kind of inner sense of what one should do—a knowing that takes one beyond what comes from a purely rational deliberation. Many of the great leaders in history relied mainly on their intuition, their hunches about when and how to act. I shall examine the role of intuition more fully in chapter 12.

Good judgment has to do with being effective but not necessarily with doing what is morally right. So it is not the same thing as wisdom. When we say that a leader is wise we mean somebody who, in addition to having good practical judgment, also has a keen moral sense. The wise leader is one who is led by conscience, by a commitment to doing what is objectively right and good. There are many leaders who can make accurate practical judgments that are for the short-term benefit of themselves and their associates but that may be grossly immoral and disrespectful of others. It would be generally agreed that Napoleon and Genghis Khan were able to make brilliant strategic and tactical decisions; but that still leaves open the question of whether or not they were wise leaders. The same applies to many of those in leadership roles in the world today, whether in the spheres of politics, or of business, or of religion.

There is one other gift leaders need in addition to an inspiring vision, an ability to take risky decisions, and good judgment. It is a keen strategic sense. This means a practical sense of how to mobilize people into an effective movement. Take the example of Pope John Paul II. He had a wonderful ability to touch the hearts of individuals and, particularly, of large groups of young people. He shared his vision with them. They went away enthused, but it was often remarked that there was little follow-up in practice. This can be explained by saying that he was generally dependent on the existing organizational structure of the church to mobilize those whom he had touched; and in many cases the local church structures did not offer these young people adequate outlets for their enthusiasm. On the other hand, we may think of Martin Luther King and of Julius Nyerere, the former president of Tanzania, both of whom combined inspirational abilities with strategic and organizational abilities. So they were able to bring about effective change.

These examples bring out how important it is for a leader of the classic type to have organizational skills, or at least to be willing to draw on the managerial skills of close associates. If this does not happen, the energy will disperse again. People whose hearts have been touched and whose minds and spirits have been inspired will fail to take the kind of effective action required to bring the vision into reality.

I have described three kinds of leader, namely, the lone leader, the emergent leader, and the classic leader. It is important to remember that there can be an overlap and a shading of one into the other. For instance, the person who is now a major leader of the classic type may have started off as an emergent leader. While working with others, this person gradually discovered the full range of his or her leadership gifts and eventually grew into a dominant and almost overwhelmingly powerful leader of the classic type.

The Power-Hungry Leader

There is a fourth type of leader. These are people who are interested in power, largely for its own sake. They do not feel fully alive and fulfilled unless they have followers, people over whom they have a certain power. They frequently have a vision, a cause they have taken up. But their vision may change, they may take up a different cause, because their primary concern is not to change the world but to exercise power over others. For this reason, people of this type may be called *power-hungry leaders.*

These leaders may have almost all the gifts of leadership I have already described: a vision, an ability to communicate and energize others, a willingness to take risky decisions, good practical judgment, a strategic sense, and organizational skills. But they cannot be called wise leaders. For they are using their gifts to further their own aggrandizement rather than putting them at the service of the community. At their worst they are extremely dangerous people. One thinks of Hitler, of Stalin, and sadly of Robert Mugabe of Zimbabwe and Hastings Kamuzu Banda, former president of Malawi.

It is only quite rarely that we see anybody who represents this type in its full purity. The examples of Mugabe and Banda bring out the point that many of these power-hungry leaders started off as leaders of what I am calling the classic type. They were visionary people, working to serve the community, and were truly inspirational for millions of people. But over the years they became more and more isolated from those who could challenge them. Gradually, they became corrupted by the power they had taken and been given.

Quite frequently political leaders are in an in-between position—somewhere on a spectrum between being power-hungry leaders and worthy leaders of the classic type. They may have an admirable vision and be genuinely devoted to the welfare of their people. But their vision may have been somewhat obscured and their dedication somewhat distorted by a long exercise of power or by a certain attachment to the privileges and symbols of authority.

I have deliberately taken my examples of leaders mainly from the political sphere, because my judgments in this area are less likely to prove controversial. Readers may choose to apply what I have been saying to those who have played a leadership role in the areas of life with which they are familiar. For instance, some may find it interesting to see to what extent these categories may apply to people like Bill Gates, George Soros, John D. Rockefeller, Mother Teresa of Calcutta, Jean Vanier, Josemaria Escriva, and Edwina Gately, as well as to the founders of various religious congregations and voluntary organizations.

Chapter 8

Styles of Leadership

In this chapter I propose to outline six different styles or modes in which good leadership can be exercised. In my opinion, all these styles are helpful, and the best leaders are able to move easily from one to the other, choosing the style most appropriate in each situation.

I trust that this practical account of the various ways in which leadership is exercised will enable readers to have a concrete understanding of the nature of leadership. More importantly, my hope is that it will help those in leadership roles to name some of the ways they are already giving leadership—thereby perhaps enabling them to exercise their leadership more effectively and with more satisfaction. It is even possible that this account of different styles of leadership may open up for present or future leaders some approaches they had not previously considered.

The Empowerment Style of Leadership

A central dimension of leadership in today's world is the empowerment of people. This can be done on a one-to-one basis by the leader's attitude of trust and respect. A key point is that the leader should look out for the gifts and talents of the members of the group, and congratulate and encourage people when they use these gifts.

Management consultants often say that positive feedback by managers to workers brings about an improvement in morale, while negative feedback brings about an improvement in performance. No doubt this is sound practical wisdom in the world of business where there is an explicit or implicit threat that if performance is not improved the workers may lose their jobs. But I have serious reservations about it as a guideline for leaders of a religious community or voluntary group. In these situations high morale is very closely linked to good performance; and blame can be counterproductive. Obviously, there is need at times for those in leadership positions to point out inadequacies and failures. But it is generally better—in terms of human relationships and even in terms of effectiveness—to ensure that such remarks are not framed as direct criticism of the people concerned.

When a leader is working with a group as distinct from an individual, the key way to empower people is by good facilitation. The heart of facilitation is to be a good listener, and to be empathetic, respectful, trusting, appreciative, and encouraging. In working with a community or organization, either in a workshop mode or in everyday dialogue, the person who acts in a facilitative role needs to keep in mind two aspects: the task that is to be done and the relationships in the group (this latter is sometimes called group maintenance). When working under time pressure, there is a great temptation to focus mainly on the task, leaving over until later such relationship issues as tension or conflict between members of the group. However, this approach seldom works well. In the long run people rarely succeed in completing the task well unless their relationships are right.

It is important that those in leadership roles be familiar with the process and skills of facilitation. Nevertheless, it is generally better, when in a formal planning session or workshop, if the official leader does not take the role of facilitator. The dialogue usually flows more smoothly if the discussion is facilitated by somebody else. In this way the official leader does not get caught up in the mechanics of facilitating the process. The leader is then free to listen to a variety of views and only to intervene when it is really necessary. But of course this will work well only if the facilitator is skillful and has been properly briefed beforehand about the issues to be dealt with. Things become very difficult if the official leader has to intervene during the meeting to explain some issue to the facilitator, or to lay down some condition the facilitator had not known about.

From a Christian point of view, facilitation can be seen as a way of opening not only the group but also the facilitator to the Holy Spirit. So, at moments when the facilitator feels stuck, it can be helpful to turn to the Spirit for light or guidance. If the members of the group are overtly Christian or open to a transcendent spiritual power, the facilitator can do this openly in the whole group; in other cases the facilitator can do it as part of his or her inner work.

It is not enough for a leader playing a facilitator role just to look for the common denominator in the group or to seek a quick consensus from the majority of the group. The facilitator needs also to be constantly looking out for the voice of the Spirit. This may come in unexpected ways—particularly from the unlikely person, for instance, a quiet, shy person who may up to then have had a very marginal position in the group.

When leaders—or leadership teams—are using the empowerment mode of exercising leadership, it is important for them to keep in mind the fundamental values stressed by Paulo Freire. These are: to trust the wisdom and experience of the group; to recognize that all are teachers and all are learners; to seek out the issues that are generative for the group, that is, those the members of the group feel strongly about; and to channel the energy of these strong feelings toward practical action. All this applies both when the group is engaged in a workshop and in the regular interactions of daily life.

It is also important that leaders take account of various points stressed by Arnold Mindell. One of these is to think in terms of managing conflict rather than imagining that it always has to be resolved or avoided. Another point is to allow—perhaps even encourage—the expression of strong feelings or passionately held viewpoints. This means that sufficient time must be allowed to deal with such feelings—and it is not easy to specify beforehand how much time will be required. Leaders should also keep in mind that it is vital that the leader or facilitator (and others too) do inner work even when in heated situations.

One of the more valuable aspects of Mindell's approach is the making of a clear distinction between roles and the people who carry these roles; and encouraging the participants to switch roles in order to see different sides of an argument. This leads on to the naming of "ghost roles"—previously unrecognized figures that have been affecting the way the group is thinking and feeling. Mindell also encourages leaders to take the side of any individuals or groups who are being targeted or scapegoated. Important too is Mindell's suggestion that one should get in touch with and give space to "the elder" in oneself—that is, the part of oneself that can resonate with the various sides and is more in tune with where the Spirit is leading the group.

Furthermore, there is wisdom in Mindell's concept of "deep democracy." This involves making space for the marginal or awkward or dissident people—the ones who seem to be disruptive and unwilling to go along with the majority view. Reaching out in this way to those who have been left on the margins of the group—or have put themselves there—in order to help them feel involved is one way of making an option for the poor.

Common Vision

So far I have been considering facilitation in general as an empowerment mode of leadership. I want now to mention two more specialized situations. The first of these is where a group works together to create a common vision. Here we can recall Covey's emphasis on the role of the leader in enabling others to find their voice. Leaders should not start off by trying to impose their own vision on others. What is needed instead is that the leader set up a process in which people are invited to share their vision and values with each other and with the leader. I note here that having a vision does not imply that one has a clear plan about what needs to be done. That comes only later. In the next chapter I will make some practical suggestions about working toward a common vision.

Even if a team or community has succeeded in working out a quite explicit shared vision, it would be a serious mistake to imagine they can move forward indefinitely on the basis of that vision. It is essential that they be willing to engage also in re-visioning in both senses of that word. At least every few years the group will need to look again at their situation, discerning the changing signs of the times. Furthermore, when a new member joins a small team, it is essential that the other members do not just expect him or her to fit in with the existing vision; they may have to start again as equals to work out their shared vision. Similarly, when a significant number of new members join an organization such as a congregation or society they should before too long be offered the opportunity to collaborate with the long-standing members in working out a new shared vision.

The second more specialized situation is where a major decision has to be taken by a group. Here it is not sufficient to have an unstructured dialogue. This is a time when a structured process of Ignatian communal discernment is very helpful, and may even be essential. It puts the emphasis on discerning the will of God through a sense of conformity with Jesus rather than in terms of a rational weighing up of the advantages and disadvantages.

This model of discernment has two particular advantages. First, everybody is asked to put forward her or his views. This means that those who might have kept silent on the issue—perhaps because of diffidence or indecisiveness or for more political reasons—are expected to give their opinion. In this way, all the members of the group know where others stand on the issue and can have a sense of which way the group is inclined to move. Second, there is far less likelihood of polarization because every member of the group is expected to put forward the arguments in favor of both sides of the question.

This model of discernment also has some disadvantages I shall spell out in more detail in chapter 13. Here it suffices to say that it requires a lot of time; and because of the fixed time slots, some members of the group may find it difficult to attain the freedom of spirit required for this kind of nonrational discernment.

For these reasons it may be appropriate at times to make use of other more creative processes to help the group in making their discernment. One may use, for instance, artistic work, or the "Frameworks for Change" workshop, or a scaled-down version of it called "The Frameworks Coaching Process," both of which I referred to in chapter 6 above.

The Nudging Style of Leadership

Although empowerment is the most obvious way leadership can be exercised, it is not the only way. One can also give leadership by finding an opportune moment to nudge people in the right direction. What I have in mind here is a situation where the leader makes some apparently small intervention that is the key that sparks off important changes.

Obviously, this requires great sensitivity on the part of the leader to the inspiration of the Spirit. Such sensitivity is evoked and nourished by what can be called prophetic contemplation. This is a kind of contemplative prayer that is not an escape from the everyday world. It is rather a style where the issues of the day are put before God, and one either dialogues with God about them or one simply holds them there before the Spirit, seeking wisdom and guidance.

The kind of deliberate key intervention I have just described is only one of the ways in which the nudging mode of leadership can be exercised. A second way is where the intervention is not carefully planned but is more impromptu. In this case the leader just follows a here-and-now intuition.

Some people are more intuitive than others—or perhaps more willing to trust such intuitive moments of inspiration. The person who takes the risk of acting on the basis of intuition learns by experience which impulses to trust. After a while, one becomes adept at distinguishing between genuine inspirations and impulses that spring from a compulsive need, such as a desire to impress the other person.

These intuitions are available to everybody, believer and nonbeliever alike. But as a Christian I am inclined to see a close link between intuition and inspiration from the Holy Spirit. I believe—though I cannot prove—that intuition is a privileged channel through which the Spirit inspires and guides us. Of course the Spirit blows where it pleases (John 3:8) and one can never be quite sure to what extent any particular inspiration is of the Spirit. Nevertheless, in the case of some intuitions the influence of the Spirit is almost tangible—especially for the person who has cultivated a close relationship with the Spirit through prayer for guidance. In other cases it may be only on looking back on the situation that one can recognize that the Spirit was at work. I shall give a more comprehensive account of intuition in chapter 12 of this book and in the appendix.

There is a third way leadership is exercised in a nudging mode. It is where the Spirit uses one's passing remark or action to spark off important changes in another person. The person who was the agent of change may have no memory of the event, and may not even have intended to influence the other person.

It is important for leaders to recognize that they may be used by the Spirit in this way as an instrument of change in the nudging mode, even though they themselves are not aware of how the Spirit was working through them. This kind of experience brings to mind Arnold Mindell's remarks about acting as an "elder": "The leader follows a plan; the elder honours the direction of a mysterious and unknown river" (Mindell 1995, 184).

The "Presence" Style of Leadership

The leader who is able to move deeply into the "eldership" space will come more and more in tune with the overall flow of life energy, both in the group and in the wider world. The effect will be that much of this person's words and actions—and even the person's very presence—are likely to have a significant positive influence on what is taking place in the group and in the world. We can recall Mindell's remark: "Unexpected solutions appear at just the right moment" (p. 195).

Those who follow Carl Jung may see these as instances of serendipity. Mindell accounts for what is happening in terms of being in touch with the "Tao," the flow of life. The Christian may interpret it as being a very sensitive instrument of the Spirit. These different explanations are by no means incompatible with each other—they may all be true.

The difference between this presence mode of leadership and the nudging mode is largely one of degree. The latter is something that occurs occasionally, whereas the presence mode comes closer to being a steady state. However, it is not an all-or-nothing affair. It may come in varying degrees and one may achieve it for a time but then lose it partly or entirely.

Indeed, it is better not to think of it primarily as something one achieves. For it is above all a gift of grace. The Christian will see it as a gift in which God allows a human person to share in the effortless creative power of God. When it happens, it makes the exercise of leadership much easier. One's energy is then used not in trying to get people to do things but in nourishing the gift of God's life and power at work within. The presence mode of leadership is an ideal those in formal or informal leadership roles should hope for, pray for, and for which they should seek to dispose themselves. The most common reason people fail to maintain this mode or style of leadership may be because they have not taken the time and space to nurture it.

The "Letting Be" Style

The wise leader knows when to intervene and when to let things be. Most of us tend to be unduly activist in our approach to life. We find it difficult to stay in a contemplative mood where we simply rejoice in the goodness all around us. But in some situations leadership is best exercised by not intervening—by leaving others the time and space to correct faults or to initiate changes.

Leaders often find themselves being pressed by members of the group to take firm action to bring about some beneficial change or to correct some fault. They need to be aware that at times it is better to resist this pressure. Of course, much hinges on their own temperament—for instance, some may be inclined to rush in too quickly, while others may be inclined to wait too long.

How can the leader know whether or not to intervene? The Christian answer is: by being sensitive to the movements of the Spirit. If we translate this into more secular terms it is probably by being in touch with the elder within.

"Letting be" means not interfering with what is happening, but it does not mean doing nothing. Being contemplative and admiring others is a positive action rather than a purely passive state. Celebration is one way of being active without interfering inappropriately. It is helpful for leaders to keep in mind the importance of celebration and to set it as one of their priority values. At times the community may be invited to celebrate some achievement or milestone in the life of one of its members. At other times the celebration may be purely internal: a little space where the leader thanks God for the gifts that have been received. Celebration, both public and private, is a crucial element in the exercise of leadership. It liberates both the leader and the community from the tyranny of activism.

The "Letting Go" Style

In addition to "letting be," the leader also needs at times to "let go." By this I mean recognizing that some project or course of action—perhaps one that may be very dear to the heart of the leader—is not working out. It has to be abandoned, or at least postponed. A useful image may be employed here. It is the difference between the pause button and the stop button. The leader who feels it would be wrong to press the stop button may find it easier to think in terms of pressing the pause button.

There are times when, despite their best efforts, leaders find themselves in a tussle for power with some members of the group. At that stage it may be good tactics to back off, refusing to escalate the struggle. This gives those on either side an opportunity to cool off and rethink their position. And it leaves the leaders the possibility of coming back to the issue at a more opportune time.

It is important that leaders acknowledge their failures when they become aware that they have done wrong or misjudged some person or situation. Leaders sometimes think they will lose their authority or credibility if they admit to having been wrong. But the very opposite is the case: people respect the person who acknowledges mistakes or failures and is willing to apologize.

People look for strength in their leaders. But, paradoxically, leaders are more effective if they are in touch with their vulnerability. From a purely practical point of view, when leaders show their fragility, people are more likely to offer them support. But there is also something deeper involved. Perhaps it is that those who are openly accepting their own weakness and inadequacy are modeling an essential aspect of what it means to be human. This encourages and empowers others. The Christian will add that those who acknowledge their frailty—and even their sinfulness—are standing in a more honest relationship with God. In doing so they are also helping to create a community rooted in sincerity, integrity, and transparency.

Inspiring Leadership

The mention of the values of integrity and transparency leads on naturally to a consideration of the sixth and final style or mode of exercising leadership—one that is extremely important: it is the inspiring mode.

In order to be inspiring one must be inspired. When people speak of somebody as an inspired leader they are generally using the word inspired as an adjective, meaning somebody who is enthusiastic, brave, generous and capable of inspiring others. But it is helpful to take the word inspired in a more literal sense, as the past participle of the verb; the leader is inspired by the Spirit. This refocuses our interest: we are now directing our attention, not so much on the person who is inspired as on the one who is inspiring the person.

Those who are in a leadership role quickly become aware of their need for inspiration. Even those who have little or no religious faith find themselves at times hoping that some transcendent power will give them light to see through the complexities of a difficult situation, wisdom to find a way forward, and courage to take difficult decisions and to carry them through.

For the Christian it is the Holy Spirit who is the primary source of inspiration. So Christian leaders have the consolation—and the difficulty—of believing that the Spirit is always willing and eager to energize and inspire them. The challenge, then, is to be open to the Spirit and to find ways of developing and fostering this openness. I will return to this issue in the final three chapters and the appendix of this book, where I deal with the topic of discernment and decision making.

However, before going on to the topic of discernment, I want to fill out what I have been saying about inspiring leadership by devoting the next chapter to an exploration of the concept of vision. This is because inspiring leaders are always men or women of vision. Their power to inspire people comes from their ability to share with others the vision that has inspired themselves.

Chapter 9

Vision and Call

All through the previous two chapters I have been using the word vision. It is time now to spell out more clearly what is meant by the word. Obviously it refers to the future, to a possible future the leader believes can be brought about largely through determined human action. But it is not a prediction or a clear plan for the future.

The most striking quality of the vision is its power. It attracts the person strongly and can generate a persevering commitment—even, at times, quite heroic action. A vision is best described as an imaginative projection from the present into the future. It derives its power through the imagination because our imagination is closely linked to our emotions. As Timothy O'Connell (1998, 105) points out, the human imagination is able to generate powerful experiences. It is not surprising, then, that strong feelings of faith, hope, and determination are evoked by a person's vision. There is also a certain joy in contemplating the vision, as well as satisfaction and a sense of fulfillment in having such an inspiring future to look forward to. If it appears that the realization of the vision is being blocked by others, this can give rise to anger.

The vision of the future is characterized mainly by the differences between it and the present. But there is room in it also for the elements of the present that are highly valued. Take, for instance, a vision a person may have of a future where poverty has been eliminated. That vision may also include the incorporation of the sense of solidarity and good community relationships that may at present be more evident in situations of poverty than of affluence.

When people are asked to spell out what their visions concretely involve they usually do so by naming certain key values. For instance, the person with a vision of a better world may say that it is a world where human rights are respected, where social justice prevails, and where people live in respectful partnership with nature and the earth. However, the vision is more than just the amalgam of all the values it embodies. The vision is greater than the sum of all these values, because it springs from the creative power of the human imagination, and this is the source of its energy. This, too, is why the vision is more likely to be expressed in terms of symbols than of rational statements.

The fact that the vision comes through the imagination and finds expression partly through symbols gives it a certain dream-like quality. (This is very clear in the Irish language where the word *aisling* refers to a quasi-mystical experience that is at the same time both a dream and a vision.) So, when we stress the importance of vision—whether that vision be a personal one or a shared vision—it would be a mistake to imagine it will be specific and explicit. Furthermore, it would be a serious mistake to believe that having a vision means not having to cope with great uncertainty.

There is a strange and interesting mixture of certainty and uncertainty about the vision. The person with the vision has a sense of knowing what it involves—and particularly of knowing what is incompatible with the vision or out of tune with it. On the other hand, there is generally a considerable vagueness about the detail of the vision.

In her book *Spiritlinking Leadership,* Donna Markham writes: "Some define the role of the leader as the individual who holds within his or her organisation some clear destination where the organisation should arrive within a given amount of time" (Markham 1999, 11).

According to Markham it is both impossible and undesirable to have such a clear destination in mind: "There can be no fixed vision, no preferred state in this time of cataclysmic change. . . . Vision, at best, is fuzzy business" (p. 12). She goes on to say that the kind of leaders she favors are ones who can navigate in a fog. They have no clear and absolute vision of the destination. They do, however, have a sense of direction—and this comes from their passionate commitment to the mission of the organization. "Mission," she says, "gives direction to vision" (p. 13).

I am not quite sure what exactly Markham has in mind when she speaks of the mission of the organization, and how this mission differs from its vision. Probably the key difference is that mission is a more active and dynamic word than vision and is therefore better suited to convey the sense of a movement from the present into a preferred future.

In fact, it is helpful to think of this movement as involving both a push and a pull. On the one hand, the sense of mission pushes one forward from the present into the future. On the other hand, the vision, being itself an anticipation of the future, has the power to call one forward out of the present situation and into the ideal future.

There are three good reasons for linking the word call with the word vision. First, exclusive use of the word vision creates a problem for people who have been blind from birth. Like sighted people, they too can exercise leadership. But it is quite likely that to them the metaphor of vision will be of no help. For blind people a much more meaningful and appropriate metaphor is that of a call. Instead of suggesting a future that is to be imagined visually, it suggests a promised future that one hears about. For the Christian, this has the added advantage that it presupposes an interpersonal relationship with God who calls us into that future.

This brings us to the second reason for using the word call alongside the word vision: call is a very biblical word. It reminds us that it is God who invites us into the future and that the future is in God's hands. A third reason for adding the word call to the

word vision is that it enables us to take account of the key concept of "prospective planning" and what has come to be called
"The Berger Methodology."

The Berger Methodology

In speaking about being called or invited into the future, I
have in mind the notion of planning from the future that is the
crucial element in "prospective planning." This concept was
developed in the 1950s and 1960s by French philosopher and
development consultant Gaston Berger. It is an approach used
in planning regional development in France. Prospective planning has been described as "the study of possible and desirable
changes in order to prepare action" (Goux-Baudiment 2001). It
"emphasizes the importance of long range and alternative thinking in strategic decision making processes" (Godet 1999).

The central point about Berger's approach is that it is "radically different from extrapolation, from simply prolonging the
present into the future" (Diagne 2004, 65). It is not a matter of
attempting to foretell what is likely to happen in the future,
on the basis of the present reality and present trends. On the
contrary, it involves visualizing a desirable future and planning
back from there, by working out the steps needed to bring about
this preferred future.

Under the name "the Berger methodology," this approach was
widely used in the 1970s in assemblies and chapters of religious
congregations facilitated by consultants associated with "The
Better World Movement." In more recent years it seems to have
fallen out of fashion. I suspect this was mainly because many
of those who took it up did not do so with full commitment or
did not carry it through properly; so they did not get the full
benefit from it.

In this book I am not attempting to deal in any detail with
the planning and management side of leadership. So I do not
intend here to go into the mechanics of the Berger methodology.
But I want to note that its central insight is very relevant to the

concept of vision—and particularly in regard to the first stages of turning a vision into reality.

As applied by the Better World consultants, the first step in the Berger methodology is to guide the group in a careful analysis of the present situation, with a view to discovering fundamental weaknesses or inadequacies that have been causing them difficulties. Having located the central difficulty the group is then helped to envisage an ideal situation several years forward from the present, in a possible future where this difficulty has been overcome. In the light of this ideal vision the group then works out detailed plans about how to move from the present into that preferred future. They do so by setting long- or medium-term objectives and more immediate targets to which they commit themselves.

There is one point that stands out when this is related to what I have already said about vision: it is that in this case the vision is consciously and deliberately constructed. This is in sharp contrast to the more usual situation where the vision that inspires and energizes people is experienced by them more as something that came to them or was given to them, rather than as something they themselves constructed.

I think the key insight of Berger is that we do not have to rely solely on the visions that arise spontaneously within us. We can also set out consciously and deliberately to design a vision. In doing so we draw on the same power of the imagination that works so effectively when the vision comes to us from some unconscious source. Whether it is spontaneous or deliberately evoked, the imaginative projection of an ideal future puts us in touch with powerful emotions and becomes a fruitful source of energy and inspiration. But, when it is done intentionally according to the Berger methodology, this vision has a particular focus. It has been designed with the specific purpose of being an antidote and remedy for the basic weakness in the present situation. That is why I think it can be particularly helpful for a group to make use of at least this key element of the Berger methodology.

Drawing on Freire, Milbank, and Covey

All that I have said about the importance and power of a personal vision and passion has to be taken in conjunction with what I have said previously about empowering others to work for a shared vision. We need to recall Paulo Freire's maxim, "trust the people"—in other words do not simply try to impose one's own vision or policies on others. This is reinforced by Covey's insistence on how important it is for the leader to work with others to construct a common vision.

On the other hand, we dare not give absolute priority to the creation of such a shared vision. Leaders who rightly commit themselves to working out a common vision with others must nevertheless give a higher priority to the demands of personal conscience. Consequently, there may come a point where leaders have to stand by their own truth. It is obvious, for instance, that if their colleagues—or the wider community—are demanding that they act in a deceitful or manipulative way, they must not yield. Even when there is no question of doing anything obviously immoral, there may be situations where leaders feel they have to resist the pressure to compromise if they are to be faithful to their personal values and vision.

At this point it is helpful to recall John Milbank's insistence on the need for aristocracy and monarchy as well as democracy. I would want to say that all leaders—and indeed all truly human persons—need to find all three of these elements within themselves. The democratic element in us is the one that inclines us to take seriously the views of others and to treat them with deep respect. This has to be qualified, however, by the aristocratic element within us. This is basically a recognition that truth and goodness are not determined solely by counting heads. There are fundamental values and truths that transcend the individual and the group and are in some sense independent of us. Our task is to search together for truth and goodness and then struggle to implement them in our own lives and in the wider society.

The monarchical element in each of us is the one that calls us to take a stand for these higher values even when we find ourselves in a minority or powerless position or "out on the margin." It inspires us to take a leadership role in trying to convince others to see and accept our interpretation of such values and the conclusions that flow from them. So we are adopting a monarchical role when we take a stand and say with Thomas More and Nelson Mandela: "This is what I believe in, this is what I live by, this is what I am ready to die for." In doing so we are challenging others to accept our leadership on the particular issue being considered.

One of the ways leaders exercise a monarchical role in inspiring others is by enabling them to hold on to the shared vision at times of low energy, or disruption, or disillusionment. Good leaders are aware of a certain pattern of ups and downs in organizations: periods of obvious success and enthusiasm are followed by dark times when people tend to become despondent; and then the pendulum may swing again to bring renewed hope. The leader can hold the organization together in the low times by reminding others of the pattern, encouraging them to endure the loss of energy, or to weather the storm. The leader reassures them that things will improve—perhaps by recalling how things worked out in the past in their own organization or that of others (cf. Benefiel 2005, 145). This is a very biblical approach: the Jews were encouraged to hold on in the dark times by recalling God's saving intervention in the past. Jesus himself did the same thing. To strengthen and inspire himself and his followers as he faced his suffering and death, he celebrated the Pasch with them, recalling the power of God at work in liberating the people from slavery in Egypt.

It is helpful to recall Covey's insistence on the role of passion in leadership. What inspires others is our commitment, perhaps even our passion, in taking a strong, clear stance. As I noted toward the end of chapter 6 above, Covey reminds us that at times the vision and commitment of the leader may be so inspiring that others buy into that vision, even if they have not been involved in shaping it. The outstanding examples of this are the nonviolent visions of Gandhi and Aung San Suu Kyi that have inspired thousands of followers. A key point here is that this stance inspires others precisely because it is done not just to inspire them but to give witness to one's dream, one's vision, one's faith, and one's life commitment.

Of course we must also recall the lines from the poem "Second Coming" by W. B. Yeats: "The best lack all conviction, while the worst are filled with passionate intensity." We may question the patrician and elitist view of Yeats about who are the "the best" and who are "the worst." Nevertheless, his words remind us that passion alone is not enough. It is salutary to remember that moral and noble leaders have no monopoly on passion and commitment. The passionate intensity of Hitler's speeches led millions of people astray. As I pointed out above in relation to the power-hungry leader, one's passionate dedication must be to truth and goodness rather than to the attainment of power over others.

Dealing with Challenge and Conflict

It sometimes happens that just when there is a convergence in a group around a common vision, one of the members has a sudden inspiration that challenges the emerging consensus. The insistence by this person on the importance of this new viewpoint poses a serious challenge to all the members of the group, but particularly to those in a leadership role. The issue then is whether the leaders and the group are open to the possibility that this interruption may represent an important truth the group needs to take into consideration.

The challenge posed by such an interrupting inspiration is especially important for us Christians. For we believe that the Holy Spirit is at work in the life of each of us. So we must be open to the possibility that the new inspiration is an interruption from the Spirit to challenge our human wisdom.

The new inspiration may come through one of the members of the group who is not part of the official leadership. The challenge it represents puts the leaders in an awkward situation. It is important that they do not react defensively, as though the person with the inspiration were just being awkward and questioning the authority of the leaders.

On the other hand, the challenge from the Spirit may be mediated through the leader or leaders themselves, calling in question what had seemed to be the consensus of the group. This situation is particularly difficult to handle, since the leaders are the ones whose special task is to work for as much consensus as possible.

The reality is that it is often those in leadership roles who have to question a view or an assumption widespread in the group. This is because, in choosing their leaders, a group often elects people whom they believe will be inspiring and challenging. Consciously, or perhaps half consciously, they expect these leaders to invite them to go beyond their comfort zone, that is, their immediate needs, fears, hopes, and desires. However, having chosen visionary leaders, the group may then pull back and try to block their initiatives, either overtly or through passive resistance.

There is one way this difficulty can be at least partly avoided. It is for the would-be leaders, before they are elected, to put forward a platform. This involves naming the various values and directions they stand for, and indicating initiatives they wish to take. These are the planks that together make up their platform. For instance, a proposed new leader or leadership team of a religious congregation might name as their priorities the taking on of a new ministry to asylum-seekers and closing down an existing ministry such as a school. In this way, the electorate have a good sense beforehand of what they are getting in choosing these leaders. When resistance arises later on, the leaders can refer back to the platform on the basis of which they agreed to take on the task.

Unfortunately, however, people are not always logical and consistent. So the leaders need to discern as they go along whether the group is still in agreement with the platform on which the leaders had been chosen. When they experience resistance, the leaders have to discern carefully whether or not to hang in there, continuing to insist on the implementation of their challenging vision. They may find at times that they have to yield, no longer insisting on some part of the platform on which they had gone forward. Flexibility and creativity are called for. A compromise position that respects the values of both sides may be proposed by the leaders—or welcomed by them if it is put forward by somebody in the group.

This may be a situation where the letting go mode of leadership is appropriate. As I pointed out in the previous chapter when dealing with this topic, there are times when a leader must admit that some agreed project or course of action is not working out, and has to be postponed or abandoned. This is a good time for leaders to recall the difference between the pause button and the stop button. If they press the pause button they still have the option of taking up the issue later on.

It often happens that, when the leaders step back, those who are leading the resistance also become less rigid, more willing to seek some acceptable compromise. Sometimes it turns out that the divergence of view was not so important. What was really going on was a power struggle between strong personalities.

There are different ways to reduce the likelihood of such a power struggle around some contentious issue. It is perhaps worthwhile recalling the processes designed by Ignatius Loyola, Edward de Bono, and Arnold Mindell, all of which I outlined in previous chapters. All three of them recognize that people may feel pulled in two opposite directions on a particular issue. Furthermore, all three of them suggest ways of ensuring as far as possible that a clear distinction is made between the issues and the personalities involved.

De Bono, in his "Six Thinking Hats" exercise, and Ignatius, in his discernment process, both suggest that all of those who have to make a serious decision should set out deliberately to explore the advantages of a particular course of action; and, in a separate procedure, explore the disadvantages. In both cases this is done in a rather measured manner, without allowing emotions to get out of control.

Mindell takes more account of the fact that people are often swayed by strong feelings rather than by rational arguments. In his model of workshop, people are encouraged to take on a role and argue quite passionately for one side or the other. Those who put the case forcefully on opposite sides of the argument are normally doing so quite authentically. But they may be speaking only on behalf of one part of themselves. They are, so to speak, putting the other part of themselves in brackets while they give full rein to emotions stirred up in them by one side of the argument. Having done so, they can then step out of that particular role. At a later stage they may well take on a role where they speak authentically and with strong emotion on the other side. The key point is to distinguish as clearly as possible between the person and the role he or she has adopted in standing for a particular viewpoint.

Mindell's process is normally done in the context of a specialized workshop. However, it is possible to make use of it also in a more everyday dialogue, provided the participants understand the concept of taking on a role and are willing to allow each other to do so.

I have been saying that leaders must accept the monarchical and aristocratic idea that all the members of a group, including themselves, have a right and a duty to stand up for what they personally believe in, even against the views of the majority. This means that the leaders have to face the prospect of conflict. In practice, then, they need to have some proficiency in the skills of conflict management. As I said earlier, it is important that they think in terms of managing conflict, rather than assuming it always has to be resolved; this means learning to live fairly comfortably with a certain degree of conflict.

Furthermore, it is helpful for them to be aware that there is more than one way of working through conflict. On some occasions the best way forward is to allow strong feelings to cool off and then seek a negotiated settlement through a reasonable dialogue. There are other situations, however, where the approach of Arnold Mindell is more effective. As I described in chapter 4, it involves having a skilled facilitator who allows the protagonists to express themselves quite passionately. The facilitator uses this release of intense emotion to draw the participants together through a kind of catharsis where differences are bridged not by rational negotiation but through shared empathy with each other's passion and pain.

Natural Leaders?

As I pointed out in a previous chapter, John Milbank maintains that some individuals are more fitted than others to play an aristocratic or monarchical role. To make such a claim may not seem politically correct. But when we look at the variety of people in any society we can scarcely deny that Milbank is right. What would be unacceptable would be the kind of conclusions some people might draw from this statement. For instance, they might give greater weight to the interests of those who are intelligent and erudite; and they might take little account of the views of people who are less educated or less clever.

Once the fundamental equality of all is safeguarded, there is no reason why those who have the attributes and virtues that fit them for leadership should hold back from using these gifts for the benefit of the community. Furthermore, those of us who are looking for good leaders are entitled—even obliged—to turn to the people in whom we see leadership potential and invite them to take on a leadership role. The chosen leaders are then entitled and even expected to give leadership. This means they should at times play a monarchical role by taking a firm stance on some controversial issue and challenging the whole group to follow and support them.

Learning from the Opposition

For the past few pages I have been emphasizing how important it is that leaders have a vision and take a stance. I now have to nuance that position. Leaders, or leadership teams, who take a firm stand on some fundamental issue should also keep in mind one of the more important points emphasized by Arnold Mindell. He insists that leaders—and everybody else—can learn valuable lessons from those who disagree strongly with them. In practice this means that, even when we are taking a firm stand on some key issue and challenging others to accept our leadership on this point, we should at the very same time hold ourselves open to the possibility that we may be mistaken. We may not have given sufficient weight to the views of others—and perhaps particularly to the views of those whose position is in direct opposition to ours.

Obviously leaders have to do a delicate balancing act between standing firmly for what they believe in, and at the same time being willing to be challenged and to change their mind. There is no magic formula that ensures this balance will be struck correctly. That is why leaders need to pay a lot of attention to the issue of discernment—a topic to which I will devote the final three chapters and the appendix of this book.

I must add, however, that those in leadership roles are not the only people who find it difficult to get the right balance between firmness and flexibility. This difficulty arises for anybody who has to make a moral decision; it is an inseparable part of being human. In the case of leaders, however, the issue is frequently more public and more pressing. So it is especially important that anybody who is in a leadership role should work and pray to be an instrument of the Spirit—an instrument who can combine docility with enthusiasm.

Chapter 10

Some Practical Aspects
of Leadership

In this chapter I propose first to address the issue of whether it is always best to have a team leadership structure rather than an individual leader. I will then go on to note some preconditions for successful leadership. Finally, I will make some suggestions about workshops or processes I believe may be of some help to those who have been asked to take on a leadership role.

Authority and Team Leadership

It is helpful to make a distinction between authority and leadership. Not all aspects of authority are covered under the heading of leadership; and there are some situations where it may perhaps be better for an individual rather than a team to exercise authority. We can distinguish between three different aspects to authority—accountability, recourse or support, and leadership.

First, there is the accountability aspect. If there is a failure to carry out the responsibilities entrusted to some authority, it is important that there be clarity about who can be called to account. In principle it is possible to call a whole team to account.

But if, as is likely, the situation is one where there has been a breakdown in communication in the team, then the individual members of the team may be passing the buck, that is, blaming each other. It may then be difficult to pin down who is really responsible for the failure. So it is useful, perhaps necessary, to have one person who has a kind of residual or fall-back responsibility and accountability. This is the person with whom, ultimately, the buck stops, and who can be called to account for the failure that has occurred or for failing to take some remedial action.

Both civil law and church law are primarily concerned with this accountability aspect of authority. That is probably the main reason why the Roman authorities resist the notion of allowing authority and leadership of religious congregations to be vested in a team of equal members. They insist on having one person designated as the person in whom authority is vested.

Secondly, there is a recourse and support aspect of authority that comes into play when individuals find themselves in trouble or confronting some difficulty. People who are in crisis or personal difficulty may find it difficult to confide even in one person and may feel quite unsafe if asked to trust a whole team. Such troubled people may even be reluctant to deal with one member of a team if they know that this member will then go back and discuss the whole issue with the rest of the team. This aspect of authority is more about personnel management than about leadership in the strict sense. In view of the troubled person's well-grounded or unreasonable fears in relation to confidentiality, this may be a situation where a whole leadership team does not need to get involved—at least not in the details of the case.

The third aspect of authority is leadership. This has come to the fore in recent years and we now consider that, for religious congregations and voluntary organizations, it may well be the most important aspect. However, this function of authority cannot easily be expressed in legal terms; so the laws of church and state tend to focus attention on the issue of accountability and responsibility, rather than on the leadership aspect.

In the past, the leadership aspect of authority was not well spelled out. But it was more or less taken for granted that the designated superior had a leadership role. This is shown by the fact that it was accepted that people in authority should inspire, encourage, and challenge those who were subject to their authority—and these are leadership tasks. In recent times we have come to believe that leadership is best exercised collectively. Hence the emphasis on team leadership.

Preconditions for Successful Team Leadership

There are two essentials if team leadership is to function effectively: the team must be able to make a clear distinction between policies and implementation; and there must be a high level of trust and good communication between the team members. Let me spell out these two points.

It is a mistake to imagine that team leadership requires everything be done collectively. What is required is that the team members make a careful and ongoing distinction between policies that are to be agreed collectively and implementation that frequently needs to be delegated to individual members of the team. Those who have undertaken to carry out the agreed policy decision have to keep the other members informed of progress. The other team members have to ensure that they do not undermine the authority of the team member to whom they have entrusted the task.

This distinction between policy making and implementation has to be made on an ongoing basis. It requires a high level of trust and good communication between the team members. When trust grows, each member comes to appreciate more and more the variety of gifts in the team. In this situation there is little need to emphasize the special extra responsibility of the team leader.

On the other hand, if there is not good communication between the members of the team, or if the trust between them has broken down or lessened, then the accountability role of the team leader comes to the fore. It is more or less essential that there be one person who can be held accountable. This person is the team leader who, in the last analysis, has the ultimate responsibility of ensuring that the difficulties are addressed. In principle this residual responsibility could perhaps be rotated among the team members; but in practice, in religious congregations and voluntary organizations, this would require so many rules and laws that the whole thing would become legalistic and unduly burdensome.

Social Conditioning

It is important for people in leadership roles to be aware that they have picked up all kinds of prejudices and assumptions from their family and social background, their education, their friends, and the people they mix with. Most of those in leadership positions in the church and its organizations come from a middle-class background; and the few exceptions may well have taken on middle-class attitudes as a result of their education and present lifestyle.

The theology of liberation challenges all such leaders to make an option for the poor. Those willing to make such an option must make a serious effort to become aware of their own biases and assumptions. Perhaps the most effective way to do this is to find some way of sharing in some degree the lives of those who are poor or disadvantaged. Coming into solidarity with the poor in this way will help leaders read the signs of the times from the point of view of the poor and the marginalized.

Currently, the members of many church organizations say they want their leadership team to take account of the viewpoint of those who are disadvantaged. One way to ensure that this happens would be to elect as members of the team one or two people who come from a less privileged background. If this cannot be done, they could choose people who are in close ongoing contact with poor people—perhaps by involvement in a project of empowerment.

An Ecological Perspective

Until quite recently—and indeed even at present—many people see concern for the environment as a particular moral value that some individuals and groups feel strongly about but that remains rather marginal for others. Such a way of looking at it is no longer acceptable. The damage being done to the world around us is so serious, and is taking place so rapidly, that the issue of care for the earth can no longer be seen as a kind of optional extra. Leaders in any sphere of life who wish to carry out their task properly must now review all their actions and decisions in the light of their ecological effects.

The pressure of immediate practical issues often weighs so heavily on leaders that it is difficult for them to give full weight to ecological considerations that may seem to them to have little immediate relevance to the matters in hand. But it is this kind of short-term thinking that has caused much of the environmental problems that are so serious today. One practical way a leadership team can ensure that ecology is given the full weight it deserves is for at least one of the members of the team to become actively involved in campaigning on environmental issues. This concern is then likely to be brought into the dialogue around all the practical issues the team has to deal with. The leadership as a whole can then find various ways to promote this value in the wider group. This can be done partly by giving support to members of the organization who have devoted themselves to care of the earth, and partly through ensuring that ecological considerations are on the agenda in relation to all major issues that come up for discussion in the wider group.

Taking on a Leadership Role

One of the more important decisions a person has to make is whether or not to take on a formal role of leadership—and if so under what conditions. I believe that nobody should take on such a role unless there is a firm time boundary—a specified time when the person relinquishes the role and becomes again an ordinary member of the group or community.

A person who is invited to take on a leadership role should, in my opinion, make a condition that she or he be part of a leadership team. There are great advantages to team leadership. The most obvious one is that the burdens of leadership are shared. But there are other benefits as well. When the team is working well, its members grow close to each other and develop a warm and tolerant regard for each other. They learn to appreciate the particular gifts of the other members of the team—and they also come to a much deeper awareness of their own strengths and weaknesses. So there can be a real excitement in working in a leadership team; and this can compensate for the stressful and burdensome aspects of the work. Each team member can receive advice and encouragement from the others about the benefits of the various skill-training workshops they have found useful. When the whole team takes part together in such workshops it usually enhances their cooperation and causes them to grow closer to each other.

The members of the team should also ensure that they are given time together to "gel" as a team, even before they begin to set priorities and make plans for when and how they will work together. They will normally need to have an outside facilitator at least for these early meetings. Individual members of the team and perhaps the team as a whole will generally need to take part in some short-term training in techniques of facilitation and planning.

The exercise of leadership is nowadays a very demanding task. So it is more or less essential that those who have taken on a leadership role in any notable way set up a program of regular supervision, where they can reflect on their work and discover how to do better in the future. It can also be very helpful if they undertake an ongoing training program in counseling skills or in group work.

I have been indicating various elements of support that are required if a person in leadership is to carry out the work suc-

cessfully over a period of years. However, all this is not sufficient. In addition to a support structure for the task, leaders need
also to establish some safeguards and support to ensure that
they survive and continue to flourish as persons. Leaders have
a particular need for friends whom they can trust implicitly. If
all a leader's close friends belong to the same organization as the
leader, issues of confidentiality can arise. So it is important that
the leader has at least one or two close friends who have no direct involvement in the leader's congregation or organization.

The other personal needs will vary from person to person. But
they should include adequate time for prayer, for vacation, for
recreation, and for some courses or workshops where the leader
goes for personal renewal and nourishment of spirit. Nowadays,
the leaders of some nongovernmental or religious organizations
find themselves being drawn more and more into an opportu-
nistic and utilitarian mind-set not uncommon among leaders in
business. Insofar as this is the situation, it is particularly important that these leaders make use of some spiritual practices to
help them to avoid such attitudes. Margaret Benefiel gives an
interesting account of various spiritual activities, drawn from
different religious traditions, used by some business leaders to
help them "stay in touch with their spiritual centre and their
moral compass" (Benefiel 2005, 147). In a forthcoming book, and
in a lecture based on part of that book, Johan Verstraeten (2005)
emphasizes the need for leaders to engage in some meditative
practice; he also suggests that leaders need to broaden their
horizons and discover news ways of thinking (and feeling) by
reading poetry.

Leaders dare not allow themselves to be available to others
all the time. There have to be clear time boundaries that are
not breached except in cases of emergency. Many leaders find
themselves stressed out and eventually burned out because
they have been working under constant time pressure over long
periods. A useful maxim for leaders to keep in mind is: "If I find
myself snowed under and unable to cope, I may be entitled to
blame others for this situation for anything up to six months; if

it continues for more than six months I have to take responsibility for it myself."

Reflection on Roles

At this point I want to refer fairly briefly to several exercises or processes that, in my experience, leadership teams have found helpful. The first of these is an exercise in which the members of several leadership teams come together to reflect and share on the different leadership roles they have taken on in the past, or in which they have found themselves.

In the case of some, their leadership gifts may have been in getting things started and taking on an organizing and planning role. The experience of others will have been mainly in a facilitating and empowering role. Some may have found themselves playing a challenging and prophetic role. The leadership experience of others may have been mainly in occupying a mediating role in a group. Finally, there are people who have exercised leadership through finding themselves in a mentoring role or acting as an "elder" in the sense described by Arnold Mindell.

It can be helpful for the whole group to divide into subgroups under the above headings. Those who have mainly been in a facilitating role all go together, and so on for the other leadership roles. The members of each of these small groups then share their experiences of the value of the particular role they have played. They may then find it helpful to explore whether they see any relationship between that specific role and one or more of the styles of leadership and types of leader I outlined in previous chapters.

The subgroups are then invited to identify ways their particular leadership role needs to be supplemented by one or more of the other roles. When all these issues have been explored in the small groups, the whole group comes together. At that point each of the subgroups in turn shares its findings with the wider group, and this leads on to a general sharing. Such a process helps to broaden everybody's understanding of what is involved in being a leader.

The Enneagram

Another exercise that can be helpful for members of leadership teams is a workshop on the Enneagram, if they are not already familiar with it. The workshop is likely to give them a lot of insight into difficulties they face in exercising their leadership role. For instance, if one member of the team discovers that she tends to be a compulsive helper, then she will realize that she may need to hold back on this inclination, and perhaps allow others to help her instead. If another member discovers that his dominant compulsive pattern is perfectionism, then he will realize that he needs to be less demanding, less fussy, and to take things more lightly. And so on, for each of the nine typical compulsive patterns that characterize different people.

Where the team members are already familiar with the Enneagram, it can be a useful exercise for them to apply what they have learned to their leadership situation. They can share with each other their struggles with their own individual compulsive patterns and ask for help from each other in moving away from these compulsive parts of their characters. It can also be helpful for the members of several different leadership teams to gather in a workshop where they have the opportunity to share with each other the ways they have found helpful in moving into greater spiritual freedom.

The Myers-Briggs Type Indicator

Nowadays, many of those in leadership or management roles are familiar with the Myers-Briggs Type Indicator. The fact that it is marketed as a professional and objective tool means that it is much more widely used than the Enneagram by those in management roles in the business world. In an earlier chapter I referred to the detailed research of Tim Bowman into the management style characteristic of a major international company. He noted that the top management had committed themselves to introducing a more person-sensitive style. But he found that they came up against one major obstacle in seeking to implement this change of direction. It was that the great majority of the present cohort of middle managers are people who, according to the Myers-Briggs typology, would be classified as strong in the "thinking" sphere rather than in the sphere of "feeling." So they are temperamentally unsuited for the task of exercising an empathetic style of management or leadership.

It can be helpful for each of the members of a leadership team to discover where they are located on the grid of sixteen different character types in the Myers-Briggs schema. They can then go on to explore the advantages and disadvantages of this type from the point of view of exercising a leadership role. Perhaps even more importantly, they can share with each other how their different character types are likely to interact with each other.

It may be more important still for them to take account of the overall strong points and weak points of the team as a whole. Are all or most of them people who look mainly at the big picture while perhaps not taking adequate account of the practical details? Are they all introverts who may not be mixing sufficiently with the community so as to be fully in touch with what is going on? Are they mainly empathetic touchy-feely types who are not getting down to serious planning and evaluation? And so on. Having answered these challenging questions, they can then go on to decide how best to build on the strengths of the team and how to compensate for its weak points.

Developing Creativity and Intuition

In chapter 6, I mentioned that present-day management consultants put a lot of emphasis on the fostering of the creativity of those in leadership roles. I gave a brief account of the "Frameworks for Change" workshop and alluded to the "Frameworks Coaching Process." Leaders who have used these processes find them useful for putting them more in touch with their creative side and with their ability to be intuitive. Furthermore, the use of these instruments helps to knit the team together. These processes can also help the members of leadership teams to deal in a nonthreatening way with sources of tension and conflict that may be operative in the team either overtly or under the surface.

More adventurous leadership teams may find it helpful to stimulate their creativity by engaging together in a dream workshop or an exercise in which they work with paint or clay or some other artistic medium. Some people even believe their spirituality can be nourished and their leadership abilities sharpened by the use of the I Ching or Tarot cards. However, if these instruments are employed, it is important that people do not use them in a superstitious way, as though they had some magical power. They are simply ways some people find helpful in bringing into the light, material that had previously been unconscious. They are possible ways to draw out one's latent gifts and inner resources.

It is imperative that people respect the reservations of those who are reluctant to have anything to do with such rather exotic approaches. What is important is that all those in leadership roles find ways to nourish their spirit, their inner strength, and their particular spiritual gifts. The most obvious way for them to do this is simply by devoting themselves to prayer, as frequently as possible during the day, both in set time-slots and in a more spontaneous way.

It is helpful also to be open to inspirations or intuitions that may pop into one's mind at the oddest of times—particularly when one wakes up in the morning or just when one is dropping off to sleep. One can stimulate the coming of such apparently spontaneous inspirations by taking time out—for instance, by walking on the beach or going for a strenuous walk on the hills.

"The Mosaic"

As I said in the previous chapter, the vision is an imaginative projection from the present into the future. If it is the corporate vision of a whole group, this may have come about in one of three ways. It may have originally been the personal vision of an inspired individual whose vision has now been adopted by the rest of the group. Alternatively, it may be a joint vision that has gradually evolved through the shared experiences and dialogue of a group of friends or colleagues. Third, it may be the vision of an ideal future that has been deliberately evoked by a group through the use of the Berger methodology. In all these cases the vision does not at first have much concrete detail precisely because it is a creative work of the imagination. When the individuals or group who have the vision are asked to spell it out, they usually do so by listing certain values that will be typical of the new reality they aim to bring about.

When a group or community set about planning how to bring their vision into reality, they may find it helpful to engage in an exercise called "The Mosaic." This can begin with a brainstorming in which the participants name the various values they believe are characteristic of the vision as they conceive it; these are written up on a board. Then each participant is invited to write down with a felt-pen marker, on a fairly small sheet of colored cardboard, the value that he or she considers to be the most fundamental of those on the list; and also to write the two or three values that are next in importance—these to be written on cards that are a different color from the color used for the value the person sees as most fundamental.

All these sheets of paper can then be used like the pieces of a jigsaw puzzle to build a pattern on the floor. The participants are invited to place in the center the sheets naming the values they see as most fundamental to the vision. Around these, the participants place the other sheets, grouping together the values they see as similar to each other. The resultant mosaic gives some indication of what the vision should look like when it is realized in the real world. This can generate some discussion about how the different values fit together. One advantage of this exercise is that it gives all the members of the group a sense of involvement in constructing and owning their common vision. However, none of this will be of much help unless it is followed up with serious planning about how the different values are to be carried into real life.

There is no shortage of books and articles about the various steps in planning. A helpful outline of a way to integrate planning and evaluation is "The Parabola Model" in Volume 3 of the *Training for Transformation* manuals (see Hope and Timmel 1995, 65–93; see also my adapted version in Dorr 1990, 118–27).

Chapter 11

Personal Discernment and Decision Making

The Context

In the first chapter of this book I quoted the prayer of the newly installed Solomon: "give your servant a heart to understand how to govern your people, how to discern between good and evil" (1 Kgs 3:9). This reminds us that discernment lies at the heart of good leadership. So I propose to devote the final three chapters of the book to this topic.

Discernment is not merely central to the exercise of leadership; it is an essential part of human living. From an early age we all learn to weigh up various options to make good decisions. We use a variety of ways of doing this. Some people just mull over the situation and let the decision emerge. Others list the arguments for and against and try to balance them against each other in a very deliberate way.

Some do their discerning alone. Others prefer to talk with a friend or adviser about important issues on which they have to make a decision. The support and challenge offered by a friend—or perhaps two or three friends together—can bring into the discernment process an element of realism it would otherwise lack. The support of friends allows one to face up to aspects one might otherwise be unable to face. The challenge of friends may help people to advert to the wounds or blind spots that limit their vision. This is the context in which I situate what I have to say about discernment in this chapter, in the next two chapters, and in the appendix.

In recent years the word discernment has become something of a vogue word among what we may call professionally religious people. It is often applied to a particular formal technique. Those who have studied and used such techniques may assume they are specialists in the discernment process. They need to remember that the vast majority of wise decisions are made by people who never advert to what process they are using—and who may never even use the word discernment.

Furthermore, it is important to note that one does not have to believe in God in order to practice discernment. Most religious people spontaneously or deliberately look to God for guidance; and Christians often see this guidance as coming from the Holy Spirit. But atheists and agnostics, relying on their human abilities, may make equally wise decisions.

Like many modern theologians, and in line with the approach of both Karl Rahner and Bernard Lonergan, I assume that Christian faith does not endow us with any new faculty for discernment. The Holy Spirit is at work in all people, whether or not they recognize that divine presence. What this means in practice is that an experience of guidance that I, as a Christian, attribute to the Spirit may also be present in a person of a different religion or none—and may be described by that person in different religious terms or in quite secular language.

Anybody who takes up a leadership role is faced with the prospect of making many difficult decisions. And those who become members of a leadership team have to learn how to make decisions together. In this chapter and the next I propose to explore the topic of techniques of personal discernment and decision making. This will provide a basis for the final chapter where I will deal with communal discernment and decision making.

Blind Obedience?

Fifty years ago members of religious communities were taught to believe that the voice of authority was the voice of God. So a spirituality of blind obedience was inculcated and even imposed on people. The members of a community or congregation were not expected to question the decision of those who had authority over them. The authorities were called superiors. The use of the word superior was quite significant: the superiors were seen as the ones who knew best what was good for the community and what needed to be done. Needless to say, this led at times to serious abuses of power. Grave damage was done both to the person who had to obey and to the person who was the superior. A further unfortunate consequence was that those who were required to give blind obedience could largely disclaim responsibility for the consequences of what they were asked to do—or for their failure to challenge practices about which they felt uneasy.

Currently this kind of blind obedience is no longer expected. Instead, it is taken for granted that one of the most important ways God's guidance comes is through the process of discernment. The new emphasis on the practice of discernment has been one of the key developments in the life of the Catholic Church since the time of Vatican II. This development has been particularly significant for religious congregations of all kinds.

At the individual level each of us is now expected to engage seriously in a personal search for God's will, and to recognize it when it manifests itself to us. Meanwhile communities and whole congregations engage in an ongoing process of communal discernment.

The Will of God

When a person says that he or she has made a discernment on an issue they generally mean something like this: "I have made a careful evaluation of the situation and of the gifts and needs of the people involved; and I have come to this decision in freedom of spirit with a sense that it is what God wants; it is God's will for me in this situation."

Many people were so oppressed in the past by the phrase "the will of God" that for them these words still evoke a sense of an imposition on them. One way to overcome this negative connotation is to think of discernment in terms of searching for one's deepest heart's desire. Some people will fear that this suggests an attitude that is too self-centered. One might respond by noting that the gospel provides a solid basis for it in the question of Jesus, "What do you want me to do for you?" (Mark 10:51). To focus on this question has the advantage of bringing out the fact that the deepest heart's desire of a truly converted person is God's desire for that person. It also locates the search for one's heart's desire within the context of a dialogue with Jesus. Another way of getting away from the negative baggage associated with the phrase "the will of God" is to recall past instances of God's generous care. One can then engage in a discernment dialogue with God by asking: "And what do you have in store for me in the future?"

The Ignatian Approach

Margaret Benefiel (2005, 55–8) gives five practical guidelines for discernment and decision making: (1) entering the decision process with a reflective inner disposition; (2) patience in the discovering of the underlying issue; (3) undertaking the hard and time-consuming work of gathering information; (4) reflection and prayer; and (5) a "contemplative pause" when the discernment is nearing its conclusion. In this book I propose to focus mainly on the last two of these five guidelines. In the present chapter and in the appendix I will examine the Ignatian approach that spells out these two aspects in considerable detail.

For those deeply involved in Ignatian spirituality, discernment is a very specific process designed to help the individual or the group to have a sense of whether or not a proposed action is consonant with the following of Jesus. Ignatius Loyola proposed two sets of rules for discernment, the first mainly for those who are struggling to reform their lives, and the second set for those who have already turned decisively to God (Ignatius, *Spiritual Exercises* nos. 313–314 and nos. 315–336; cf. Brackley 2004, 46 and 133–4).

My concern here is with the kind of discernment to be made by a person who is already converted, in basic harmony with the divine will (cf. Ignatius, *Spiritual Exercises* nos. 315–336). For such a person, the issue is that of choosing between two options, both of which are morally unobjectionable. The point of the discernment is to decide which of the two is more compatible with the fundamental conformity of the person to God's will. The person making the discernment brings each of the options in prayer before God—and more specifically before Jesus.

Ignatius proposes three ways of discernment. The first two involve reliance on feelings as the criterion for choosing one course of action over another. The third is a more rational process in which one weighs up the arguments on either side. Ignatius indicates that the third method of discernment is a fallback, to be used if one's attempt to discern on the basis of feelings does not produce a clear sense of which option is the right one to choose (*Spiritual Exercises* no. 177; cf. Rahner 1964, 95–6 and 164). I shall focus here on discernment on the basis of feelings partly because this is the preferred mode for Ignatius but also because there can be a lot of confusion in relation to it.

The spiritual feelings of consolation and desolation play a central role in the main discernment process described by Ignatius (*Spiritual Exercises* nos. 175–176 and nos. 313–336). Tad Dunne says: "Spiritual consolation . . . is an experience of feeling centred, at peace within, full of confidence in God" (Dunne 1991, 162). His description of spiritual desolation is: "We feel dark inside, troubled, anxious, restless, lazy, sad. Or we may feel giddy, scatterbrained, skittish, frivolous, silly. We feel out of touch with our centre, separated from God, and alone" (p. 163). I would want to add an explicitly social and political component to this account. People may also be in desolation when they feel a sense of paralysis in the face of major evils like debt, abuse, slavery, human trafficking, drugs, and AIDS.

A person using Ignatius's process of discernment must be able to recognize these feelings. Such a person must also learn to link these feelings of consolation and desolation to specific proposed courses of action. This means learning to know when a sense of consolation can be interpreted as an indication of divine approval. The hope is that in prayer the person will have a sense of consolation about one option, a sense that this proposed line of action fits in with the mind of Jesus. When the person considers taking the other option it evokes a sense of desolation or distaste.

There are various nuances to be added to what I have said in the previous paragraph; otherwise it would represent an oversimplification of Ignatius's account of discernment. The first point to note is that Ignatius holds that a person making a decision may have a special kind of experience called "consolation without preceding cause." This "uncaused" consolation provides the criterion for Ignatius's first mode of discernment. He maintains that a decision arising from this kind of discernment is utterly convincing because the consolation clearly comes directly from God. The exact nature of this kind of consolation and how it operates are quite controversial and technical issues that I will examine in the appendix to this book. In this chapter I will focus on the more usual kind of consolation—the one "caused," that is, which follows on our thoughts, or our acts of will (cf. Brackley 135).

Ignatius holds that "caused" consolation does not always come from God and is therefore not always a guarantee one is making the right choice, even in the case of a person who is advancing from what is good to what is better. There is need, therefore, for a good deal of spiritual sensitivity in order to note whether the pattern of the whole experience, including the period of its "afterglow," is one of lightness and peace; or whether, on the other hand, there is any disturbance—any entrance of something evil or less good—during or after the experience. If some disturbance has crept in, this may be an indication that the original consolation did not come from God and therefore that the proposed choice is not in accordance with God's will (*Spiritual Exercises*, nos. 333 and 334; cf. Buckley 1991, 230–1; Brackley 2004, 136–7; Doran 1990, 57–8).

Affective Conversion

It is evident that this whole method of making a discernment can be trustworthy only if one's feelings are in line with one's basic moral and religious orientation. We cannot assume this is the case. We must not presume that all those who are morally and religiously turned to God are therefore capable of making a good discernment on the basis of their experiences of consolation or desolation. Many people have been so wounded by abuse of one kind or another that their whole affective system has become deadened or mixed up. Many others are affected by personal or group biases, which means that their feelings can lead them astray.

When these wounded or biased people become morally converted, or when they turn to God in religious conversion, their affectivity or sensibility is not automatically healed and straightened out. This means that their feelings may be pulling in the opposite direction to the way they have committed themselves to go. Furthermore, a person making a decision may have a serious blind spot, a failure to recognize or admit to a prejudice distorting the discernment process.

There is need, then, for what has come to be called "affective conversion." This involves a quite radical conversion and reorientation of human sensibility. It means that one no longer experiences serious resistance at the feeling level to the commitment one has made to God and to the good. We should note, however, that affective conversion is not an all-or-nothing affair. It can come in varying degrees. (On this whole topic see Tyrrell 1996, 26–7; Doran 1990, 51–2; Doran 1981, 145–6; Buckley 1991, 232).

We can perhaps find a scriptural basis for affective conversion in a text from St. Paul's Epistle to the Romans (12:2): "Let the renewing of your minds transform you, so that you may discern for yourselves what is the will of God, what is good and acceptable and mature." When Paul speaks of "minds" here he is not limiting the word to just our mental capacities, but envisages the whole person. So we can understand Paul to be suggesting that in order to discern the will of God the whole personality, including one's affectivity, needs to be converted or transformed—turned away from evil and toward the good.

The effect of the conversion of affectivity is that the feelings are brought into line with, and now support, the person's basic orientation—or reorientation—that is constituted by moral and religious conversion. Borrowing a phrase from Ezekiel, one might say that the person's heart of stone has been replaced by a heart of flesh (Ezek 36:26). Consequently one's feelings can now be a reliable guide in making choices—even more reliable, at times, than one's thinking. At this point one discovers the truth of Pascal's famous dictum: "The heart has its reasons which the reason does not know."

As I have said already, the reorientation of affectivity does not always come about as soon as a person turns to God. In fact it is quite difficult to attain. This has serious consequences. As Lawrence Murphy points out (1976, 46), those in whom it has not taken place "are not able to make fruitful use of the experience of consolations and desolations in the discernment of spirits."

There are times or situations when people's affectivity is so wounded or mixed up that realistic discernment may require a certain amount of professional counseling or therapy. A counseling session may help them to realize and acknowledge what they really want to do, as distinct from what they might like to think they want.

I recall a woman in a group affirming very strongly that she wanted to be closer to her family. The counselor said: "And what are your hands saying?" The woman looked at her hands and realized that the more strongly she spoke of her desire to be close to the family, the more strongly she was unconsciously pushing them away. She realized that her first priority had to be to get some time for herself; only then could she really be available to her family. I suspect that many dutiful or devoutly religious people are as out of touch with their real desires as she was. When people in such situations wish to make authentic decisions, it may be more helpful for them to begin by undertaking some nondirective counseling rather than by turning at once to prayer.

Spirituality and Psychology

As I pointed out in chapter 2 above, the Jesuits' Official Directory of 1599 made a significant shift shortly after the death of Ignatius: its authors played down the importance of discernment on the basis of feelings of consolation or desolation. They gave priority instead to the more rational style that Ignatius had seen as a kind of "fallback" approach when the other one failed (cf. Brackley 2004, 151). As Harvey Egan puts it, there was now a distrust of discernment on the basis of consolation or desolation in favor of an excessively rationalistic interpretation of discernment on the basis of weighing up the reasons for and against (Egan 1976, 151). Egan notes that this led to a divergence between the early Ignatian commentators and the more recent ones who have returned to the original Ignatian position.

It is scarcely a coincidence that the return to Ignatius's emphasis on the importance of feelings came at around the same time as the development of humanistic psychology in the secular world. Over the past forty years there has been a notable convergence of spirituality and psychology; and the Ignatian renewal is a significant aspect of this wider movement.

The presupposition of the Ignatian approach to discernment seems to be that behind the everyday consciousness of each person there is some kind of deeper self that plays a privileged role as an instrument of enlightenment by God—provided the person has been converted not only religiously and morally but also at the level of sensibility. One gets in touch with this deeper self in prayer. It comes to consciousness in the form of spiritual feelings of consolation or desolation. These feelings are seen as a normal way in which one can discover or check whether a proposed course of action is in conformity with the will of God. This fits in very well with humanistic psychology, particularly with the views of those who are in the Jungian tradition. They too suggest that we tend to live on the surface for much of the time. When we need guidance or a sense of direction in our lives we have to open up to a deeper part of ourselves.

Formal or Informal Prayer?

I would like here to make a comment about the Ignatian model of discernment—more by way of addition than of criticism. It is important to make a clear distinction between the key insight of the Ignatian approach and the particular procedure Ignatius proposed. The key insight is that a very effective way to engage in the discernment process is by adverting to feelings of consolation or desolation. The proposed procedure is the two periods of prayer in one of which the person envisages not taking the proposed action and, in the other, taking the action.

I believe that as well as the procedure proposed by Ignatius, there are other ways of using his key insight about discernment. I think it would be a mistake to assume that it is only—or even primarily—through a formal period of prayer that one comes to sense whether or not a particular course of action is in conformity with the will of God and the following of Jesus. Undoubtedly prayer is vitally important. The most obvious way to engage in personal discernment is to pray about the issue. This usually works quite well. Through prayer we can sometimes achieve a certain inner freedom, an ability to rise above the hassle, confusion, and worry that may have been blocking us. Prayer is especially helpful when the difficulty in making the decision is a moral one—for instance, a reluctance to let go of selfish interests. Through prayer we can become more open to the needs of others—and especially to the cry of the poor and the oppressed.

Nevertheless, formal prayer is not always the best way to get in touch with the deepest and most authentic desires of one's heart—especially when this is in the context of trying to make a decision. The very expectation of getting light and an experience of consolation or desolation seems sometimes to create a kind of block, so that the person remains blank.

Furthermore, it is not easy for some people to lay aside a certain veneer of piety that can bring an element of unreality or even falseness into their prayer. There are many who have been deeply hurt by somebody in authority and who, as a result, are living in a wounded state. When such persons come before God in prayer their piety may tell them it is necessary to "forgive and forget." Consequently, they may not allow themselves to acknowledge the extent to which the hurt remains. So they may make decisions that seem quite sincere, but they may never quite get around to acting on them. This is because these decisions did not truly reflect their real feelings and therefore did not come from the deepest part of themselves.

Many people find that some of their best discernment takes place not in formal prayer and not in dialogue with others but simply by taking space. One way to do this is to go for a long walk in some wilderness or remote place during which one can leave aside one's regular occupations and preoccupations. By distancing oneself in this way and getting out from under the pressure of the decision that has to be made, the pieces may fall into place quite naturally. One may then have a clear sense of consolation associated with one of the options about which one has to decide. The point here is that one is using the key insight of Ignatius without adopting the particular procedure he proposed.

I am not suggesting that prayer plays no part in this type of discernment. There are other forms of prayer than the set periods of formal prayer recommended in the standard Ignatian process. There are times when one's heart and mind may be more effectively raised to God when walking on the hills or by the sea than when kneeling in a chapel. The Spirit blows where and when the Spirit wills. So, it is important to be open to the possibility that the movements of the Spirit so central to discernment may come outside of formal times of prayer—and even on the most unexpected of occasions.

Chapter 12

Intuition as a Basis for Discernment

The authorities on Ignatian discernment have written a great deal about feelings. But they seldom refer to intuition, perhaps because Ignatius does not refer to it. This is a pity. I think that, as a development of the Ignatian approach, it may be useful to explore intuition as a channel of the Spirit and a way in which discernment can take place. My reason for wanting to explore this topic is that most people have had the experience of being struck by an intuition that turned out to be an accurate guide to what they ought to do.

Here I note that intuition, like discernment, is a universal human phenomenon. So, in suggesting that intuition may be a channel of guidance from the Spirit, I assume that guidance through intuition may come not merely to Christians but also to non-Christians. In that case it is likely to be described by them in secular language, or in the idiom of a different religious tradition.

Many people have the experience of finding that, having mulled over a decision for some time without being able to make up their minds, they suddenly realize that their decision has been more or less made in an intuitive way and they have only to ratify that decision. It is as though a deeper part of themselves had done the discerning—and done it much more effectively when their more logical thinking part had been switched off.

That stepping back from normal thinking and planning seems to leave space for the deeper part of the person to send its inspirations welling up into consciousness.

Going for a long walk or run is one way of switching off excessive reliance on a purely logical-rational-discursive approach to decision making. Going to sleep is another way. Some people find that as soon as they wake up in the morning they somehow know what needs to be done about an important issue that had been at the back of their minds. A particular direction seems to be presented, inviting them to ratify it. Their experience indicates that decisions that emerge in this way are almost always the right ones.

Those who have learned to trust and follow their intuition find that, even without going to sleep or going out to the hills, they can often have immediate access to a less discursive and more intuitive part of themselves. It is simply a question of noticing that an intuition has come into consciousness, and of trusting this intuition. There is a very close connection between the noticing and the trusting; for if one does not trust such intuitions, they quickly slip out of consciousness and one is no longer aware of having intuitions.

Two Types of Intuition

Intuitions about decision making seem to come in two different forms. The first kind come as new insights that open up options one had not thought of previously. They do not have the quality of being a conviction about one just right way to go. Instead they offer one or more new possibilities worth considering. Strictly speaking, these are insights but it seems appropriate to call them intuitive insights or intuitions because of their more mysterious and unexpected quality—particularly because they come when one has stopped pushing or trying; and also because they spring up in a context where one is being prompted to take action.

The particular value for discernment of this kind of intuitive insight is that it leaves one with a new and different kind of spiritual freedom. By opening up a wider range of options than one had envisaged previously it liberates one from being stuck with a restricted choice between taking a particular action or not taking it.

This kind of intuition is a new insight about a possible direction one might choose. This new possibility still has to be evaluated, alongside the previously recognized options. This evaluation can be done by using the Ignatian method of inference in terms of consolation or desolation. If that does not produce a clear sense of the rightness or inopportuneness of this new option, one may fall back on the third Ignatian method, a more deliberate and logical weighing up of the arguments for and against.

The second—and more interesting—form in which an intuition about decision making comes is as a conviction about the right decision to make. It has a certain quality that inclines one to know that a particular course of action is the right one to choose. The intuition still leaves one free. One may reject this knowledge for one reason or another—but fundamentally because of a failure to trust it. Looking back on some wrong decision, people frequently say: "I knew I should have done that, but I just wasn't prepared to take the chance."

As experienced, this kind of intuitive conviction feels like a strong invitation to the person to take a particular action or move in a specific direction. It does not, however, compel the person. It leaves one fundamentally free. The person must have sufficient trust to follow this mysterious call.

Can We Trust Intuition?

I believe that intuitive insights and intuitive convictions are not a separate source of knowledge and conviction, independent of the regular process by which we gather data, gain insight, discover truth, and decide what to do. On the contrary, they occur at the point where all these processes are seamlessly integrated and where we come closest to being fully aligned and authentic persons. Just as an iceberg remains mostly below the surface of the water, so in the case of intuition the regular processes of knowing and deciding take place in a very compacted and perhaps symbolic form, mainly below the surface of consciousness, and through the picking up of all kinds of subliminal signals. Then the resulting intuitions burst into consciousness ready-made, seeming to come from nowhere.

Since intuition is not independent of the rest of us but rather springs from a deep place in the integral person, it is subject to some of the inadequacies we experience in our regular knowing and deciding. The person who is not fully integrated—in other words, the person who is not converted at the affective level—may not be intuitive at all. If new convictions do pop into this person's consciousness they are unlikely to be trustworthy. And if new possible courses of action spring to this person's mind they may well be inappropriate, perhaps even bizarre. This is because the different parts of the person are pulling in opposite directions.

Even the person who is affectively converted and pretty well integrated may still be the victim of ignorance of relevant information. Furthermore, this person may still be subject, to some extent, to personal or group prejudices; and some of the wounds of the past may not be fully healed. In other words, affective conversion may not be total. And it is only to whatever extent the person is fully integrated, fully aligned, that this person is capable of receiving intuitions that can be relied on.

All this means that intuition is not an infallible guide to action. On the other hand, intuitions are generally trustworthy provided the person is affectively converted, aligned, and integrated. They do, however, require a certain amount of checking out. This checking is mainly a matter of ensuring that the intuition is really coming from a deep place within and that it is experienced as an expression of the person as centered, aligned, and at peace.

The account of intuition I have given here still leaves some important questions unanswered. What is the relationship between intuition and the feeling of consolation that plays a central role in Ignatian discernment? More particularly, is there any link between intuition and the Ignatian "consolation without preceding cause"? An exploration of these topics helps one to understand whether and when one may trust intuition. But such an exploration takes one into some deep and quite technical cognitional theory and theology. For this reason I have left it to be treated in the appendix to this book.

Intuition and the Holy Spirit

Whenever Christians are dealing with an intuition, or looking for one, it is helpful for them to hold in mind and heart the conviction that the Holy Spirit is at work in people's hearts, offering inspiration and guidance. Until quite recently this word guidance seemed to be used almost exclusively by those in the Pentecostal or charismatic traditions. It is important to bring it back into mainstream Christian spirituality. We can expect guidance from the Spirit, we can ask for it, and we should recognize and welcome it whenever it comes, whether at a time of formal prayer or in any other time when the Spirit chooses to touch us.

For me, guidance from the Spirit is associated particularly with one's intuitive capacity rather than with one's more obviously logical and reasoning faculties. It is not easy to say why one should give a privileged place to intuitions welling up from the depths or popping ready-made into one's mind. I am inclined to think there is more room for the Spirit to work when one is not so concentrated on maintaining control. In any case, it is largely a matter of learning by experience to trust one's authentic intuitions. Over time one comes to recognize the particular quality that invites one to recognize and trust a genuine intuition, distinguishing it from an ungrounded impulse or an off-the-wall idea. I believe that a genuine intuition can in fact be seen as an inspiration from the Spirit.

During the past ten years I have run many workshops that focused on intuition, and this has shown me that different people experience intuition in different ways. In the following paragraphs I will share my own experience on this issue. I think it is likely that some will find an echo of their experience in what I have to say. And my hope is that those whose way of experiencing intuition is different from mine will at least be stimulated to turn their attention to their own intuitive capacity and articulate for themselves how it works for them.

When a new light pops into my mind about some course of action I might take, I try to respond in gratitude and let in the possibility that it may have come from the Spirit. Then I endeavor to use a process of inference to discover whether it is a genuine, trustworthy intuition I ought to follow. I do this by looking closely at the source, or channel, of the invitation to action that has come into my mind. If it comes as a bright idea, I think of it as coming from my head. In this case I am aware that it may be followed quite quickly by another bright idea that suggests I go in the opposite direction! So I have learned to be rather cautious in acting on such ideas.

On the other hand, if the source (or channel) of the invitation to action is my heart or my gut, I find it more trustworthy, because it is characterized by a steady and reliable quality. For me the heart and the gut are frequently sources or channels of authentic intuition. As Childre and Martin (2000, 27) say: "The 'heart' isn't only open to new possibilities, it actively scans for them, ever seeking new intuitive understanding." A person's heart seems to be the center from which relational impulses spring—ones linked to feelings of compassion and caring for other people or, on the other hand, feelings of dislike or distaste. The gut seems to be a center from which spring those deeper impulses associated with personal survival and feelings of well-being: a sense of threat and insecurity or, on the other hand, of safety, groundedness, harmony, and deep peace.

At this point, one finds a link between intuition and the range of feelings Ignatius of Loyola calls consolation and desolation. In this connection, it is worth noting that John Carroll Futrell, one of the main authorities on Ignatian discernment, refers to "deep peace at the bottom of the heart" that he contrasts with what is going on "at the top of the head" (Futrell 1972, 164–5).

I think the usage of the words heart and gut is not entirely metaphorical. Some recent scientific studies suggest that the heart, and other parts of the body, have their own kinds of intelligence that seem to be at least partly independent of the brain (cf. Childre and Martin 2000, 10, 13, 15; and Pearmain 2001). Furthermore, it is hardly a coincidence that, in various cultures, different human reactions and energies are linked to different locations in the body. In the Indian traditions, for instance, the heart and the gut are considered to be *chakras* or energy centers in the human body. All this suggests that we may take quite literally Pascal's statement: "The heart has its reasons which the reason does not know."

The fact that I am stressing the importance of the heart and the gut does not imply that I undervalue the contribution of my head, that is, of the logical-discursive and obviously rational part of me. In my case there is very little likelihood that I will fail to use my head, since I spent sixty years developing and relying on it. In recent years I have come to believe that, in my case, the discursive-logical-reasoning abilities function best when I rely on them not so much to show me *what* I ought to do as to show me *how* to do what my heart or my gut invites me to do. It is often a matter of letting my heart lead me (cf. Dunne 1995, 168). I could even say that I feel myself called to give my heart its head!

My experience of working with others has led me to believe that the situation may be somewhat different for other people. Some people experience intuition as coming solely from the heart, while for others it seems to come solely from the gut. And there are people for whom the mark of intuition is a particular kind of eager quiver or tremor throughout the body.

The mere fact that an impulse comes from the heart or the gut is not a guarantee that it is an authentic intuition. There are some people who act very spontaneously and at times impulsively, being led by their heart (or their gut) in a totally unreflective and uncritical way; and this leads them into a lot of difficulty. It seems that these are people who have relied on their heart or gut center to the neglect of their head center. For them, the fact that an impulse comes from the heart or the gut may not be a good indication that it is an authentic intuition. When it comes to discernment, it may be important for them to make more use of their head center to monitor the impulses that come from the heart or the gut.

Developing One's Intuitive Powers

One of the most effective ways I have found of developing my intuitive powers is by engaging in one or other of two rather similar processes—one called "The Transformation Game" and the other called "Frameworks for Change." For me, one of the advantages of these workshops is that they offer an interesting and fruitful combination of professional facilitation with the warm, spontaneous support and challenge of friends. Furthermore, in both of them there is a quite explicit emphasis on the spiritual aspects of the human journey and human discernment—and they both invite one to be open to inspiration from Spirit or the Beyond. This is one of the ways they differ from a purely psychological kind of counseling. Their overt spiritual orientation provides a context in which friends can advert to, and engage in dialogue about, spiritual experiences and issues they might have overlooked, or undervalued, or never dared to talk about, or even to articulate for themselves.

Both these processes give an important place to the exercise of intuition. Those who take part in them learn to distinguish genuine intuition from the kind of impulse that arises from some psychological need such as the desire to please people. They learn to differentiate between a fully human response and a mere reaction. They also have the opportunity to explore what kind of checking out they need to do when an intuition comes. They find that it is not a matter of moving into a logical calculating mode but rather of going inside to discover where the intuition is coming from. In this way the processes help the participants experience more clearly the difference between making a decision based on an intuition and one based on a more logical-discursive process.

Many people assume an intuition is something that comes to them uninvited and unexpectedly. They imagine that the most they can do is simply to hope an intuition will come when they most need it. So their role is to be passive and receptive. Through repeated engagement in these workshops, they find that they can consciously access the intuitive part of themselves and actively look for an intuitive response to a question. In effect, then, these workshops help people realize they can at times evoke an intuitive response in themselves.

When one seeks to access one's intuitive power, or invites an intuition in this way, there is no guarantee one will get an immediate response. This is because a person's intuitive capacity does not come under the direct control of the reasoning part of the person. However, one can learn to be more open to intuition, and then one is more likely to get a response to one's request for an intuitive response. There is a delicate balance to be found between inviting intuition and trying to force it.

As I said already, it is important to be sensitive to intuitions when they do come. This involves learning to notice how easily one can close off or smother an intuition just as it is beginning to come to full consciousness; also how easily one can dismiss an authentic intuition because of insecurity or because there are no convincing rational grounds for following it. When an intuition comes, one should try to trust it and act on it. Furthermore, it is helpful to look back on, and review, the way one makes decisions, taking note of which energy center the impulses came from and the results of acting on the basis of different impulses. In this way one can learn by experience the characteristic quality of an authentic intuition.

Leaders who succeed in being in touch with their intuition are likely to discern more effectively and to make better decisions. For our intuitive capacity is a privileged instrument used by the Holy Spirit in guiding all of us on life's journey. It is a particularly valuable resource for those in a leadership role, a channel by which the Spirit gives them direction and guidance.

Chapter 13

Communal Discernment and Decision Making

In the past, authority and obedience played a central role in binding together religious congregations, societies, and communities. With the abandonment of the older notion of blind obedience, the process of corporate discernment has become crucial because it is now the essential cement that holds the membership together. The members of congregations and religious organizations explore their distinctive charisms and traditions by discerning together. In this way each congregation or society is able to work out its own mission statement (or some equivalent articulation of its fundamental purpose); and appropriate policies are then formulated. Discernment is also used in devising suitable structures and in the selection of leadership teams. These teams in turn generally employ a communal discernment process in making their major decisions.

In recent years a number of congregations and societies have begun to make a formal link between discernment about policies and discernment about leaders. They ask prospective leaders to outline their vision and the kind of policies they favor; and to indicate what leadership gifts they have to offer. This provides a basis for more realistic group discernment both about policies and about a leadership team that can implement them.

Approaches and Difficulties

Communal discernment can be a rather informal process where a large or small group explores an issue together and works toward a consensus. On the other hand, it can have a much more formal structure where various options are explored, prayed over, amended, and voted upon. A more formal procedure is generally adopted when there is question of revising constitutions or adopting official policies or mission statements at general chapters or assemblies.

The parliamentary model of debating, proposing amendments, and voting has certain basic values of which the key one is that it is democratic. But when it is applied to deeply spiritual issues many people find it uncongenial, rather deadening, and at times quite exhausting. It can also be somewhat divisive since the emphasis on voting tends to polarize people and strengthen the sense that there are winners and losers.

Aware of these difficulties, good facilitators or process consultants generally try to create a sharing and prayerful atmosphere. This enables the drafting of documents to run more smoothly. Sometimes it works so well that the participants feel enriched by the whole process. But, even at its best, this approach does not address the core difficulty, namely, that the group is being asked to articulate the fundamental purpose and mission of their institute through the use of a process that is primarily discursive; and consequently they seldom feel the process to be a deeply spiritual experience.

Over many years I have been involved, both as a participant and as a facilitator, in helping to draft mission statements and policy documents of various kinds. My experience is that it can often be a very burdensome task—even when situated within the context of a sharing and prayerful group process. Furthermore, it tends to give a privileged place to those who are articulate and nimble with words. Less weight is given to those who are slower or more reserved in articulating their views—or who are not so proficient in negotiating about what goes into a consensus document. This means that at times the statement adopted may not fully reflect the beliefs and commitments of some influential members of the group, namely, those strong, silent types who are admired and looked up to not because of what they say but because of their dedication and practical wisdom. Furthermore, the consensus may sometimes be based less on a real meeting of minds and hearts than on exhaustion and impatience to move on.

The Ignatian Model

Some groups make use of an Ignatian model of communal discernment. This brings prayer very explicitly into the process of decision making: the members of the group are given time to pray about proposed courses of action; time is then given for sharing with the whole group the fruits of this personal prayer. John Futrell (1970b and 1972) and Jules Toner (1971 and 1974) have both given detailed accounts of the various stages of the process, so I do not propose to repeat them here. However, since discernment is a key aspect of leadership, I think it may be useful to make some comments on the process, pointing to some of its advantages and also some of its difficulties.

It is important to note that the Ignatian model of communal discernment is not an alternative to personal discernment. On the contrary, it requires that each of the people engaged in it makes a personal discernment on the issue. But it is equally important to note that the process is not one of working out a compromise between a number of individuals, all of whom have made up their own minds on the issue.

What the process calls for is that the individuals pray over the issue, noting whether this brings consolation or desolation. Then, deliberately holding back from making a personal decision for or against, they all share with the group the outcome of their individual personal discernments; that is, they share whether they experienced consolation or desolation when they set the proposed action in the context of the following of Jesus.

This provides the raw material for the communal discernment. Consequently, there is no question of bargaining or arguing. Instead, the issue is being explored through the sharing of spiritual feelings. This is its key advantage.

One of the other advantages of the use of the Ignatian model of communal discernment is that it greatly reduces the likelihood of polarization. For it asks each member of the group to go away and pray about the reasons for not undertaking a particular course of action and then come back and share the feelings that came up for them; then, in a separate session, each is invited to pray about the reasons in favor of taking the action, and then share the results of their prayer. This means that everybody shares on both the case for and the case against the proposed action. In this way the members of the group are invited and expected to set aside their prejudgments and look anew and objectively at both sides of the issue.

A further advantage is that in this approach all the members of the group are expected to indicate where they stand on the issue. This helps to clear the air. It enables the group to avoid a difficulty that often arises when an issue is being debated in the conventional (parliamentary) manner—a situation where a fairly small number of people dominate the discussion while the others stay quiet; and nobody really knows where the silent ones stand on the issue until it comes to a vote.

Disadvantages

Perhaps the biggest disadvantage of the process is that not very many groups are both able and willing to make use of it properly. William Barry has noted that in fact it has not been used very much in recent years. He suggests that this is because not many groups have attained the "prerequisites" that will enable them to engage in a true process of Ignatian communal discernment (Barry 2001, 162–3). He then goes on to give a valuable account of his experience of working with groups to help them attain these prerequisites. The kind of prerequisites he has in mind seem to be mainly the overcoming of fears and old hostilities or irritations, and the gaining of courage to share freely the spiritual experiences that have come up in prayer. Another prerequisite for the successful use of this kind of communal discernment is experience of personal discernment according to the Ignatian model (pp. 163–74).

A further difficulty with this Ignatian model of communal discernment is that the demands of the timetable force members to fit their personal prayerful discernment on the issues into fairly tightly organized time slots. Some people find this quite acceptable. But for others it is artificial and constricting—especially since they are being asked to figure out in prayer the advantages and disadvantages of major issues they would like to mull over or sit with for a long time.

When properly used, the process can be very cumbersome and can take a long time. This means that those in charge of the agenda of the meeting need to confine its formal use to major issues. And there may be disagreement about which issues are sufficiently important to merit the use of this lengthy process. In fact the setting of the agenda can be a major problem. Some members of the group may feel that the choice of issue or the way it is worded is biased or weighted in a particular direction.

Futrell (1972, 185–9) offers some suggestions about ways of generating proposals for deliberation. His proposals are very rational—so much so that there is a danger that the Ignatian emphasis on feelings could get lost. Furthermore, the process he prescribes for the rewriting of documents (Futrell 1972, 177–8) seems to assume that the participants will move back into a quite discursive mode of dialogue. On the other hand, Virginia Varley (1996, 89–94) gives an account of an Ignatian-style communal discernment process that incorporates more imaginative elements such as the creation of "a history line" and moving toward a common vision.

The Ignatian process was designed primarily for yes or no decisions. This means that it is not so easy to use it in situations where there are several different options. And it would be very cumbersome to use it for the drafting of a mission statement or a carefully nuanced policy document, except perhaps at the stage of final ratification. Even then, some members of the group might feel dissatisfied that the formulations they favored were not put forward as options.

Even though the Ignatian process is not intended to operate at a purely discursive and rational level, it is by no means easy to ensure that the group sharing gives full value to the convictions and deep spiritual sense of those members who are not very articulate at the verbal level. Indeed Dean Brackley seems to consider it unlikely that a communal discernment can be carried out successfully on the basis of the experience of consolations and desolations. This is indicated by the following passage from his highly regarded book on discernment: "Discernment through reasoning is especially appropriate for communal decision making. For while we cannot expect subjective experiences of consolation and desolation to coincide, members of the group can appeal to the same objective data in searching together for the most reasonable thing to do" (Brackley 2004, 148–9).

The conclusion that emerges from all of the above considerations is that in situations where the personal discernment of the great majority of the group results in a real convergence of opinion, the process of communal discernment based on consolation and desolation works very well. But, where there are major differences between the individuals after their personal discernment, the members of the group have to fall back on a more rational-discursive style; and then there is a danger that the sharing can become a debate or even descend into a contentious argument.

A Role for Intuition and Inspiration

Probably the most important aspect of the whole Ignatian approach to discernment is the high value it sets on feelings of consolation and desolation. Without in any way wishing to play down the importance of such feelings, I think it can be helpful in making a communal discernment to also pay particular attention to people's intuitions.

As I suggested in the previous chapter, individuals engaging in a personal discernment process may draw on their intuitive powers. They can give a lot of weight to the hunches or intuitions that well up spontaneously from the heart or the gut or some other deep place within them about the direction they ought to take in life or about the rightness or wrongness of some proposed course of action. They can even at times evoke such intuitions. This involves putting themselves in touch with that place or space within them where their intuitive powers seem to be located or centered. Intuitions, I suggested, can be a basis for discernment and good decisions.

Furthermore, people who are deeply spiritual and who are also quite intuitive often have a sense that, for them, intuition is a channel through which they receive guidance from the Holy Spirit. Quite frequently they can experience such intuitions as graced moments of inspiration—not, of course, infallible but certainly deserving to be taken very seriously.

However, when it comes to communal discernment, it is much more difficult than in the case of personal discernment to give full value to intuition as a basis for discernment and as a channel by which the Spirit can guide our decisions. This applies especially when the group is using the recommended model of Ignatian communal discernment. The need to fit the process into a group timetable means that the available time is often felt to be either too short or too long. If it is too short, the individual may not be able to get in touch with that deep place from which intuition springs. If the time is too long, there can be a loss of energy and of focus, so that doubts creep in. In effect, then, people may feel almost forced to fit the discernment into a structure that is somewhat rational rather than one congenial to the inclinations that come from the heart or the gut.

In the light of this difficulty, there is something to be said for trying out another approach—one designed with the specific purpose of being congenial to intuition. Perhaps the most obvious of these is the "Six Thinking Hats" process designed by Edward de Bono that I outlined in chapter 6 above. At one stage in his process, the members of the group are invited to put on red hats as a reminder that at that point their task is to share their feelings and hunches about the issue to be decided.

Some groups may be willing to try out another process—one that can be used not merely when some yes or no decision is to be made but perhaps particularly when the members of a congregation or organization are discerning about drafting a mission statement or policy document. In these circumstances it can be helpful for them to make use of a process that lends itself to the evoking of declarations of purpose and commitment that well up intuitively and spontaneously from some deep place within individuals who have a deep commitment to the mission of the organization.

What I have in mind is a situation that has two basic elements. The first is that one member of the group, speaking from the heart or the gut, without prior planning, spontaneously articulates his or her deep convictions and commitments in relation to the identity or purpose of the organization. The second element is that this passionate declaration of belief immediately rings a bell for the others in the group, to such an extent that they find themselves ready to adopt it as part of a mission statement for the whole group.

An Interesting Experience

Some time ago I had an experience that led me to believe such a model of discernment is feasible. I was invited to take part in an intense six-day process in which the members of a spiritual community set out to clarify and name the fundamental purpose of their institute and at the same time to face up to difficult issues about their structure and leadership.

There was a group of about one hundred twenty people involved. They did not engage directly, as most religious groups would have done, in the complex process of drafting a mission statement and policy documents. Instead, they immersed themselves in a simulation, that is, a kind of game that mirrors the processes of everyday life—and that does so in a heightened and focused form. In this case they used a process called "The Planetary Game." Through the simulation they explored deeply personal issues in a manner that put them in touch with their most heartfelt convictions. The process helped them to distinguish between such deep convictions on the one hand and on the other hand the "bright ideas" or conventional assumptions sometimes aired in parliamentary-style discussion of issues. Furthermore, it ensured that their exploration of the overall purpose of their institute was done in and through their tackling of issues that touched each of them in a deeply personal way.

The current leaders of the group courageously and publicly addressed the real-life dilemmas they were encountering in their exercise of leadership. Other members of the community were equally honest in sharing on the key issues touching their lives. There was very little formal dialogue in the sense of a direct exchange of views between the participants. The main emphasis was on a public but utterly personal exploration of issues by individuals who had immediate experience of confronting these issues. The exploration was guided by skilled facilitators who helped people to bare their souls in public on how they were agonizing about, and responding to, vital personal issues—such as how they were experiencing their roles as leaders. The topics they were dealing with were not just personal ones. They were issues of deep and immediate concern to the whole community. This gave an air of realism and relevance to the whole procedure. Furthermore, the very experiential quality of the process caused it to be intensely interesting and engaging for everybody present.

It was fascinating to see how the airing of the burning issues at the personal and interpersonal level had immediate implications at the institutional level. Questions about authority structures and models and styles of leadership were approached pragmatically from below. The articulation of the purpose of the community was allowed to emerge largely through an exploration of the experience of people who had been involved in leading and guiding it—and the experience of other members of the group who had firm convictions about where the community ought to be going and who had tried to have their views accepted by the group.

The wholehearted immersion of the participants in the process evoked a number of spontaneous personal statements that were, literally, heartfelt articulations of the spiritual purpose of the community as a whole. What struck me very forcibly was that at times these impromptu declarations were inspired statements that touched the hearts of all who were present and carried great weight with all who heard them. Some of these inspired proclamations of what people stood for, and of the values they believed in, were a more powerful and accurate articulation of the community purpose than could have been arrived at through a long, communal drafting process.

By Acclaim

In the light of this experience, I think some religious congregations, societies, or organizations might find it helpful to experiment with a discernment process that would be neither discursive nor Ignatian. Like the Ignatian approach it would recognize that the personal spiritual search and journey of the individual is organically integrated into the process of articulating the common purpose of the group as a whole. But it would differ from the Ignatian approach in putting a particular emphasis on intuition and on spontaneous heartfelt declarations as authentic expressions of the human spirit—and as privileged channels of inspirations from the Holy Spirit. So the process would give a high value to statements or remarks that well up spontaneously in members of the group, putting words on their deep convictions and commitments. Furthermore, the members of the group would be open to the possibility that such statements could be inspired articulations of key aspects of the group mission.

Picture a situation where a group have immersed themselves in an intense group process dealing with issues of passionate concern to all of them. In such a setting, one or more of the members is likely to have a moment of inspiration. Speaking straight from the heart—or from the gut—they put forward an expression of their fundamental convictions and beliefs. These are intensely personal statements rather than attempts to articulate a balanced consensus policy. Yet such proclamations may strike a chord for everybody there. Using Ignatian language, one might say that all, or almost all, the participants experience a sense of consolation as they resonate with what has been said.

The result could be that the inspired declaration of one individual is acclaimed by the whole group. It might become the basis for a major decision by the group. Alternatively, or additionally, it might become the basis for a mission statement adopted by the whole group.

If we really believe in the power of the Spirit, then it should be normal to expect this kind of thing to take place. Something like it seems to have happened in the very early church at the first Council of Jerusalem (Acts 15:6-29). It is also worth noting that until quite recently one of the ways a new pope could be chosen was "by acclaim"—where the Spirit inspires the whole group to shortcut the long process of election. Why then should we not invite the Spirit to sometimes make use of such an acclamation process in our work on mission statements and policies? After all, religious congregations often adopt certain inspired statements of their founders as their guiding principles. Should we not, then, ask and expect the Spirit to be just as evidently active among us today?

I am not suggesting this is the only way a group should seek to generate mission statements and declarations of policy. But such inspired and acclaimed statements would be a valuable counterpoint to the mission statements drafted through a more conventional process. The crucial point is that there should be room for articulations of purpose that come directly and evidently out of the hearts and guts of the participants rather than through a heavy and perhaps heady discursive process. At their worst, such expressions of deeply felt convictions springing from the heart can be unbalanced and unduly fervent. But at their best they have a quality that marks them as truly inspired—a flavor or aura that indicates they are products both of the spirit of the group and also of the Holy Spirit.

Creating the Right Atmosphere

The hope of evoking such inspired statements is not the only reason for engaging in the kind of process I am suggesting. Perhaps more important is the fact that it could help the members of a community or assembly experience a real sense of communion with each other. It could foster an ability and willingness to share deep spiritual feelings and movements of the spirit, and a readiness to listen respectfully and openly to others who share their experiences of movements of the Spirit. These are among the key prerequisites that William Barry believes are essential if a community is to engage fruitfully in the Ignatian process of communal discernment—and that he finds missing in many communities (Barry 2001, 162ff.). I would add that they are prerequisites not merely for the use of the Ignatian process but also for any effective process of joint discernment.

Part of the responsibility of the organizers of any gathering where important decisions have to be made is to design a process that will foster the right atmosphere of openness, listening, and sharing. If the group has already reached that stage, they may be ready to engage in the Ignatian communal discernment process as outlined by Futrell and others. If they are very closed and polarized, then they may need some quite elementary listening and faith-sharing exercises. If, however, they are fairly open but have not yet reached a stage where they can fruitfully engage in the Ignatian process, they may benefit from the kind of process I am suggesting. It may awaken them to the possibility of new inspiration. Even if no inspired declarations emerge from the process it may at least help the participants to identify and deal with some of their blocks and inhibitions. In this way it may dispose them for involvement at a later stage in the Ignatian type of communal discernment.

This process may be particularly helpful in situations where many of the participants already have taken up strong positions regarding important issues—for instance, whether a prestigious school or hospital should be closed down or handed over to others, or whether a development agency should move out of some countries in order to concentrate on other regions. In such situations it may not be realistic to ask people to adopt a stance of complete openness or what Ignatius would call "indifference." However, if the group were to engage in the kind of exercise I am suggesting, it is likely they would be touched and moved by seeing each other struggle with deeply personal issues that may have nothing to do with the looming decision that is divisive in the group. This could generate a respect for the way the Spirit is working in each member. It could lead to a new openness to believing that the Spirit might be saying something to the whole group through the individuals who have been on the opposite side of the fence.

Even then, the organizers might feel the group is still not ready to engage in the standard version of the Ignatian communal discernment. In that case they might postpone the formal consideration of the divisive issue. They could recommend that over a period of days, or even weeks, the members of the group, while continuing work on other topics, should strive in their times of formal and informal prayer to gain a greater degree of freedom of spirit in relation to the contentious issue. They might suggest that each of the members of the group engage in an extended and less formal version of Ignatian personal discernment on the issue, by bringing the pros and cons of the issue before God and before Jesus in their formal prayer and in their quiet time, while begging the Spirit for freedom of spirit, for inspiration, and for the kind of consolation that would promote fruitful discernment.

It is a mistake to assume that it is possible to guarantee a successful outcome to communal discernment by the adoption of any particular process or method. What is needed is a respect for where the group as a whole is at, and for each individual within it. This respect is the basis for a judicious choice of approach and of processes that will lead the group toward a greater degree of freedom of spirit and of openness to the guidance and inspiration of the Holy Spirit.

Appendix

"Consolation without Cause"

When writing chapters 11 and 12 of this book I was dealing with the difficult and controversial topic of personal discernment. I wanted to write in a manner the general reader would find readable and interesting. So I omitted any detailed account of what Ignatius of Loyola calls "consolation without preceding cause." I also refrained from referring to the views of various scholars whose views supported what I was saying or who took a different approach. However, in this appendix I am attempting to give a more comprehensive and somewhat technical treatment of "consolation without cause" and to indicate how it relates to intuition.

What is "Consolation without Cause"?

According to Ignatius of Loyola "consolation without preceding cause" can come from God alone (*Spiritual Exercises*, nos. 330 and 336). Consequently, a discernment made while this experience is fully present is quite reliable and does not require further authentication. The first issue I want to consider here is: what is the nature of this kind of consolation?

There is a wide diversity of views among Ignatian scholars on both the nature and the frequency of this experience (see, for instance, Toner 1982, 244 and 291–313; Toner 1991, 320–2; Green

1984, 130–4). Karl Rahner takes "without cause" to mean without an object. So he understands "consolation without cause" to be an utter receptivity to God, a nonconceptual experience of the love of God (Rahner 1964, 134–5; cf. 137 and 153).

Bernard Lonergan (1972, 106) accepts this formulation of Rahner. In working out what this involves, Lonergan focuses on the key text in Romans 5:5 where St. Paul says that "the love of God has been poured into our hearts by the Holy Spirit which has been given to us."

There are different views about how Lonergan understands this text. Robert Doran (1993, 60 and 62) suggests that it refers to an immediate experience by us of God's unconditional love for us. Michael Vertin (1994, 30) suggests that "there is no real difference between my experience of the gift of being loved and my experience of being in love unconditionally." Tad Dunne (1995, 169–71), reflecting on his own experience, maintains that what Lonergan has in mind is not an immediate experience by us of God's unconditional love for us but rather an experience of our love for God. Dunne argues that our conviction that God loves us is not an immediate experience of God's love "as such" but actually involves a judgment of value about our own worth, leading to a judgment of fact that God loves us without condition. This judgment is a "faith judgment," an act of trust, based on the evidence of our love for God and on our realization that "God is not waiting for our response before coming to us. God is the love with which we love" (p. 171).

I have come to accept that Dunne's account comes closest to my own experience. However, I think it may be helpful to nuance it a little. Drawing on an important study by Frederick Crowe (1959 and 2000), I suggest that our love as experienced in this situation is not primarily love as reaching out to God or to others but love as what I may call "resting in"—love evoking peace, serenity, and a sense of fulfillment and gratitude. This is a human experience of ours, rather than strictly a direct experience of God's love as such—though it is of course, like everything else in our world, a created participation in the divine life. Patrick Byrne (1995, 149) describes it in poetical terms: "being undifferentiatedly immersed in love, like a crystal clear vessel immersed in a crystal clear sea." Dunne (1995, 172) suggests that the metaphor of an overflowing fountain is particularly apt; and he goes on (173) to liken it to the love of those who have grown old together and whose love overflows into children, neighbors, and the wider society.

I want here to comment on the specific phrase "without preceding cause." Does this necessarily imply that the experience comes from God with no secondary causality at all? Yes and no. Yes, in the sense that all genuine love is gratuitous, a free gift that is not caused by anything we or anybody else does. No, in the sense that we may have to some extent disposed ourselves for the gift. The special experience of having unconditional love welling up in us may be quite closely related to some process that has been taking place in us below the level of consciousness; but that unconscious process is not, strictly speaking, the cause of the experience. The main point is that the unpredicted and mysterious way this overwhelming love arises leads one to *experience* it as "without cause."

Can it have an Object?

The second point I wish to consider is one that is raised by Rahner's explanation of "consolation without cause" as meaning "consolation without an object." Lawrence Murphy (1976, 42, footnote 46), refers to a study by Leo Bakker that disagrees with Rahner's explanation. The case against Rahner's view is based on an important letter written by Ignatius in 1536 to a Sister Rejadell. In the letter Ignatius says: "It often happens that Our Lord moves and forces us interiorly to one action or another by opening up our mind and heart, i.e., speaking inside us without any noise of voices, raising us entirely to His divine love, without being able to resist His purpose even if we wanted" (Ignatius 1996, 133–4, no. 15). This text is commonly interpreted to refer to the experience of "consolation without cause" (cf. Toner 1982, 312). And it seems to indicate that for Ignatius the phrase "without cause" is not the same as "without an object."

The account I have just given of the nature of "consolation without cause" goes some way toward resolving this disputed issue. It would suggest that in the first and primary "moment" or aspect of the experience one is not reaching out to any particular object of choice, but simply experiencing oneself as resting in love. There may, however, be situations where one's response has a second "moment"—an aspect of reaching out to a particular object or choice.

As experienced, this reaching out in love by making a specific choice may on certain occasions be more or less inseparable from the sense of being immersed in love. This could happen, for instance, in a situation where an important decision has been weighing on one's mind and it now seems resolved. It could also happen that a person might be strongly drawn to respond lovingly in some way that had not previously occurred to the person, but that he or she now finds to be almost inextricably linked to the letting in of love.

The making of a distinction between these two "moments" in one's love seems to fit quite well with the advice of Ignatius in his "eighth rule" that one should "distinguish the time itself of such actual consolation from the following," and with Rahner's distinction between the experience itself and its "penumbra." At the same time it enables one to explain how Ignatius could write a letter indicating that one can have an object in mind when experiencing "consolation without cause." In this letter Ignatius would be thinking of a situation where the specific object of choice is so closely linked to the "consolation without cause" that the two are more or less inseparable in practice.

Only Love for God?

A third question arises here: is it possible for somebody who has little or no explicit relationship with God to experience what Ignatius calls "consolation without cause"? I have no doubt the answer is yes. This implies that the experience can be described in more secular terms than those used by Ignatius. In taking this view I am encouraged by Bernard Lonergan's remark to the effect that the experience of the love of God poured into our hearts is interpreted differently in the context of different religious traditions (Lonergan 1972, 241; cf. Doran 1995, 157; and Byrne 1995, 149). In our modern, rather secularized culture it may be that the experience is articulated by the use of some or all of the following terms: a sense of deep abiding peace, fulfillment, love, joy, gratitude, benevolence, or loving-kindness.

This leads on to a closely related question: what is the relationship between affective conversion and religious conversion? Bernard Tyrrell maintains that the highest degree of affective conversion brings the peace and joy of being in love with God (Tyrrell 1996, 26–7). I am not quite sure about this formulation. How would it apply to a Buddhist who may be affectively converted to an exceptionally high degree while making no reference to God?

Tad Dunne's account seems preferable. He says that people who are affectively converted are those "who let their heart take the lead." He refers to a statement made by Lonergan in 1977 where he said that affective conversion is defined as "commitment to love in the home, loyalty in the community, faith in the destiny of man." Dunne does not differentiate between religious conversion and affective conversion by making the former the highest level of the latter. He says rather: "among those whose heart leads, some let their love of God take priority over everything else"; these latter are people who are religiously converted (Dunne 1995, 168). In the light of this position we might say that religious conversion occurs when a person who is already affectively converted recognizes God or some ultimate value that is effectively God under another name; and when that person consciously submits to this God, and chooses to take God as his or her highest priority.

Three Separate Methods?

The fourth point I wish to consider is the relationship between the three different methods of making an "election" or choice described by Ignatius (*Spiritual Exercises*, nos. 175–88). Ignatius says that in the first method God moves and attracts the will to such an extent that it follows what God shows it, without any doubting, or being able to doubt (no. 175). The second method involves a discernment on the basis of the more regular kinds of consolation and desolation; and the third method is based more on what Ignatius sees as "natural powers," that is, reasoning and deliberating.

Toner (1982, 12-3 and 1991, 325) makes an important preliminary point: that discernment of spirits is not the same thing as discerning God's will; the former is only one component in the latter. So we cannot take for granted that the first method or "time" of election always involves an experience of "consolation without cause." Some Ignatian scholars do hold that this is the case; but not all the authorities agree on this point (cf. Brackley 2004, 278, note 4). Karl Rahner seems to assume such a link and goes on to say:

> The first method is the ideal higher limiting case of the second method and the latter itself includes the rationality of the third as one of its own intrinsic elements. The third method is the less perfect mode of the second . . . and itself seeks to rise beyond itself into the second kind of Election. (Rahner 1964, 106)

Harvey Egan adopts a similar position:

> [I]n the ideal Election there is an interpenetration or fusing of the Three Times which the Exercises explicate as three distinct Times only for clarity. In the concrete, however, the Three Times are not three distinct ways of finding God's will, but actually aspects of one core experience and Election in which all three aspects are present in varying degrees of intensity. (Egan 1976, 152)

Brackley, having summarized the views of Rahner and Egan, goes on to maintain that Ignatius "considered each of the three methods to be autonomous and reliable in its own right"; but he adds that the second and third methods "can be used in tandem" and that it is desirable that each of these two methods be used to confirm the other (Brackley 2004, 152). Other Ignatian authorities hold that the three modes of discernment are not intended to be quite independent of each other. Michael Buckley (1991, 231) says, "neither affection nor rational intentionality is self-justifying; it is their unity which must obtain and in which one level is critically judgemental of the other."

I refer here to what I said about affective conversion in chapter 11 above. I said there that it is not an all-or-nothing reality; it can come in varying degrees. I suggest now that the experience of "consolation without cause" can come only to those who have been affectively converted to a high degree. The mere fact that a person is already converted to a high degree at the level of *moral* commitment does not mean this person can experience "consolation without cause." To have this experience one must also be converted at the *affective* level; and the degree to which one is so converted determines the degree to which one can let in and fully experience the love of God.

Those whose affective conversion is less total can experience God's love in a less intense way. Therefore they can have the more regular kind of consolation—the one that is "caused," meaning that it follows on our thoughts, or our acts of will. To adopt this approach is to agree to some extent with Rahner about the connection between the two kinds of consolation; for him, "consolation without cause" is the ideal higher limiting case of consolation; and he holds that what is called "consolation with cause" is a lower degree of the same reality.

In this connection, Brackley (2004, 138) makes an interesting point. He maintains that it is not just in the case of "consolation without cause" that there is a disproportion between the experience and what has gone before; he holds that every experience of consolation is disproportionate to what preceded it, as its apparent cause. I think this is true and it links with my earlier statement that every genuine experience of love is quite gratuitous. This bolsters the case for seeing "consolation without cause" as a limit case of a feature characteristic of all genuine consolation (cf. Egan 1976, 140, on the "First Time Election" that he would presumably see as linked to this type of consolation).

However, there is a big question about the conclusion drawn by Rahner and Egan. They seem to be saying that the fundamental basis for all real discernment is ultimately consolation without cause—suggesting, perhaps, that it is present in some low degree in the more regular experience of consolation. This implies that, far from being a rare occurrence, the experience of consolation without cause is quite frequent and normal.

One suspects that, in his account of consolation without cause, Rahner (followed by Egan) is focusing not so much on discovering what exactly Ignatius was saying as trying to interpret Ignatius in a way that accords with Rahner's own fundamental theology of our experience of God. In any case, Toner (1991, 320–2 and 1982, 301–13) puts forward a very convincing case for disagreeing with Rahner and Egan on their interpretation of Ignatius; he shows that there is no evidence that Ignatius believed that consolation without cause is the fundamental basis for all genuine discernment.

On the question of whether or not consolation without cause is a frequent occurrence, Toner (1982, 306–13) suggests that it is by no means a frequent and ordinary experience and so he disagrees with Rahner's view. However, the crucial issue is not its frequency but whether it is the fundamental basis for all true discernment; and on that issue Toner's view seems preferable to Rahner's. In that case, it is hardly necessary to speculate about how many people God touches with an experience of consolation without cause or how frequently it takes place in any individual—and one might even wonder whether it is somewhat impertinent to do so.

What about "the third way," namely, the use of one's natural powers of reasoning and weighing up considerations on one side and the other? Is there any relationship between it and the kind of discernment and choice made on the basis of feelings of consolation or desolation? I see a clear link between them because we must think of the human person as an integral whole. A person is not just a spirit or soul inhabiting a body and employing two or three different kinds of "machinery"—a logical-discursive-rational machine at one time and a machine that weighs up feelings of consolation or desolation at another time.

The person who is acting rationally is by no means leaving feelings aside as irrelevant. This is especially so when it comes to deliberating about choices. Our choices are based on values. And our values are "carried" by our feelings. So when we are deliberating about what to do, we are not in fact acting like a computer uninfluenced by feelings.

Ignatius attributes the feelings of consolation and desolation to "the good spirit" and "the evil spirit." Most Ignatian writers nowadays do not exclude the possibility that some kind of external spirits may be at work. But their understanding of consolation and desolation is a more psychological one; they focus on the feelings rather than on some external cause. When one takes this approach it is easy to see that all three of the modes of discernment are closely related to each other.

Intuition and Consolation

The final point I want to consider here is whether there is a relationship between consolation and intuition. Against the background of my earlier account of the nature of the two kinds of intuition, I suggest that there is. The experience of satisfaction and fulfillment that are an integral aspect of genuine intuitions can be seen as consolation in the Ignatian sense. This is particularly the case regarding the type of intuition that, in chapter 12 of this book, I called "intuitive convictions."

This kind of intuitive conviction may be seen as arising from a compacted process in which various subliminal signals have been picked up and there is an evaluation of evidence, namely, of different values that are carried by the person's feelings. In this case the evidence for choosing one course rather than another is filtered and evaluated mainly at a symbolic level rather than in the full intellectual pattern of experience. The evaluation takes place in such a compacted and almost instant manner that the conclusion seems to pop ready-made into consciousness.

I tentatively suggest that a person's intuitive conviction of the rightness of a particular choice may, on some occasions, be an instance of what Ignatius calls "consolation without preceding cause." I am not claiming this is true of every intuitive conviction we get. But I think that there are times when such a conviction may be so strong, may feel so right, and may be accompanied by such an overwhelming experience of unconditional love that it may in fact be an instance of "consolation without preceding cause."

I said in chapter 12 that, though this kind of intuition pops into one's mind in a mysterious and unpredictable way, it is actually the fruit of a process that has been taking place below the level of consciousness. So the conviction has arrived into consciousness without any preceding *conscious* cause; but it does spring from an *unconscious* process. How then can it ever be called "consolation without cause"?

In reply, I note the following statement of Ignatius in his second rule: "I say without cause: without any previous sense or knowledge of any object through which such consolation would come, through one's acts of understanding and will." His statement indicates that when referring to a cause, what he has in mind is some conscious human action. It does not, I think, exclude the possibility of a prior unconscious process; that possibility simply did not enter his mind.

There is no need to assume that God is intervening in some miraculous way when one experiences an intuitive conviction of the rightness of some course of action. God's action in the world is through secondary causes. Though Ignatius had acute psychological insight, he did not have access to modern knowledge of the workings of the unconscious. So, for him, the consolation that came without reference to prior conscious operations could rightly be described as being "without preceding cause."

However, a difficulty arises at this point. Though this kind of intuition is without a conscious cause it is certainly not "without an object." For it is a conviction about a particular course of action one strongly senses to be the right one. This is not an insuperable difficulty. For, using Rahner's language, we may say that a choice made on the basis of such a compelling intuitive conviction may be a choice made in the "penumbra" of "consolation without cause."

I think there is a slightly more accurate way to express what is happening. Recalling a distinction I made earlier, I would say that such an intuitive conviction belongs not to what I have called "the first moment" of upwelling love (that involves "resting in" the love), but to its "second moment" that may be a reaching out to some person or course of action.

The practical conclusion to be drawn from all this is that even a very powerful intuitive conviction that is almost inseparable from an overwhelming experience of love is not necessarily and infallibly correct. There is the possibility that the person's choice in this situation, as elsewhere, may be mistaken or inadequate due to ignorance of some relevant facts, or due to bias at the personal, or group, or general level. Nevertheless, there is a strong case for trusting the intuition. This is because, normally, it represents the best this person can do at this moment—provided, of course, that the person has been converted affectively.

One should not act blindly and impulsively on such conviction-intuitions. There is need for some checking. But this is not normally a matter of trying to repeat the whole process in a deliberate and fully logical step-by-step manner at such a slow speed that one has time to reflect consciously on each step. For this kind of checking still leaves one at the mercy of ignorance and unconscious bias; and there is the added risk that the rich meaning of the symbolic material, together with the values carried by feelings, may become impoverished or distorted when one tries to translate them into clear and distinct ideas.

In this context it may be helpful to recall what Toner has to say about the "first time of election" described by Ignatius "when God our Lord so moves and draws the will that without doubting, or the power of doubting, the faithful person follows what is shown . . ." (*Spiritual Exercises,* no. 175). Toner is perhaps the most meticulous of all the Ignatian scholars. He argues, against other Ignatian scholars, that even this "first-time" experience "with its spontaneous certainty of what God wills, is only data for a discernment by critical reflection on it" (Toner 1995, 11–3). The person needs to check whether the conviction is truly indubitable and whether it has been accurately grasped and remembered. Applying this to what I have been calling conviction-intuitions, we may say that the checking the person has to do before acting on the intuition is mainly a matter of making sure that this intuition truly springs from one's deep center and is not just a reaction rooted in some neurotic need; one needs also to advert to the possibility of ignorance or of bias due to inadequate affective conversion.

Bibliography

Adler, Mortimor J. (2005). "The Democratic Revolution" http://radicalacademy.com/adlerdemocraticrevolution3.htm downloaded 30 May 2005.

Arendt, Hannah (1977). *Between Past and Future: Eight Exercises in Political Thought* (enlarged edition). Harmondsworth: Penguin.

Barrett, Richard (1998). *Liberating the Corporate Soul: Building a Visionary Organization*. Butterworth: Heinemann.

Barry, William A. (2001). *Letting God Come Close: An Approach to the Ignatian Spiritual Exercises*. Chicago: Loyola Press.

Benefiel, Margaret (2005). *Soul at Work: Spiritual Leadership in Organizations*. Dublin: Veritas; New York: Seabury Books.

Bloom, Allan (1968). *The Republic of Plato*, translated with notes and an interpretative essay. New York: Basic Books, Inc.

Bowman, Timothy James (2004). "Spirituality at Work: an Exploratory Sociological Investigation of the Ford Motor Company," unpublished doctoral thesis of the London School of Economics and Political Science (used with the permission of the author).

Brackley, Dean (2004). *The Call to Discernment: New Perspectives on the Transformative Wisdom of Ignatius of Loyola*. New York: Crossroad.

Brown, Raymond (1970). *The Anchor Bible: The Gospel according to John*. Garden City, New York: Doubleday.

Buckley, Michael J. (1973). "Rules for the Discernment of Spirits" 19–37 of *The Way Supplement* No. 20, Spring 1973.

——— (1991). "The Structure for the Rules of Discernment" 219–37 of *The Way of Ignatius Loyola: Contemporary Approaches to the Spiritual Exercises,* Philip Sheldrake (ed.). St. Louis: The Institute of Jesuit Sources.

Byrne, Patrick H. (1995). "Consciousness: Levels, Sublations, and the Subject as Subject" 131–50 of *Method: Journal of Lonergan Studies* Vol. 13, No. 2 (Fall 1995).

Chambers, Mary Catherine Elizabeth (1885). *The Life of Mary Ward (1585–1645)* 2 Vols., London: Burns and Oates.

Childre, Doc and Martin, Howard (2000). *The Heartmath Solution*. San Francisco: Harper.

Collins, Sean (2005). Personal email citing early Franciscan documents.

Conn, Walter (1986). *Christian Conversion: A Developmental Interpretation of Autonomy and Surrender*. New York/Mahwah: Paulist.

Covey, Stephen (2004). *The 8th Habit: From Effectiveness to Greatness*. New York: Simon and Schuster.

Crowe, Frederick (1959). "Complacency and Concern in the Thought of St. Thomas." *Theological Studies*, 20 (1959), 1–39; 198–230; 343–95. Reprinted in *Three Thomist Studies* (supplementary issue of Lonergan Workshop Vol. 16), Boston College, 2000.

De Bono, Edward (1990). *Lateral Thinking: a Textbook of Creativity*. Harmondsworth: Penguin.

——— (2004). *Six Thinking Hats*. Harmondsworth: Penguin.

Diagne, Souleymane Bachir (2004). "On Prospective: Development and a Political Culture of Time," in *Africa Development*, Vol. XXIX, No. 1, 2004, pp. 55–69 (downloaded 18 June 05).

Dollard, Kit (2002). Anthony Marett-Crosby, and Abbot Timothy Wright, *Doing Business with Benedict: The Rule of St Benedict and business management: a conversation*. London and New York: Continuum.

Doran, Robert M. (1981). *Psychic Conversion and Theological Foundations: Toward a Reorientation of the Human Sciences*. Chico, California: Scholars Press.

——— (1990). *Theology and the Dialectics of History*. Toronto: University of Toronto Press.

——— (1993). "Consciousness and Grace" 51–75 of *Method: Journal of Lonergan Studies* Vol. 11, No. 1 (Spring 1993).

——— (1995). "Revisiting 'Consciousness and Grace'" 151–59 of *Method: Journal of Lonergan Studies* Vol. 13, No. 2 (Fall 1995).

Dorr, Donal (1990). Integral Spirituality: *Resources for Community, Justice, Peace and the Earth*. Dublin: Gill and Macmillan; Maryknoll: Orbis Books.

——— (2002). "Bringing Ethics and Spirituality into Business" 195–213 of Pontifical Council for Justice and Peace, *Work as the Key to the Social Question: The Great Social and Economic Transformations of the Subjective Dimension of Work*. Vatican City: Libreria Editrice Vaticana.

Dunne, Tad (1991). *Spiritual Exercises for Today: A Contemporary Presentation of the Classic Spiritual Exercises of Ignatius Loyola*. San Francisco: Harper.

——— (1995). "Being in Love" 161–75 of *Method: Journal of Lonergan Studies* Vol. 13, No. 2 (Fall 1995).

Egan, Harvey D. (1976). *The Spiritual Exercises and the Ignatian Mystical Horizon*. St. Louis: The Institute of Jesuit Sources.

Fleming, David L. (1978). *The Spiritual Exercises of St. Ignatius: a Literal Translation and a Contemporary Reading*. St. Louis: The Institute of Jesuit Sources.

Freire, Paulo (1985). *Education for Critical Consciousness* (revised edition). London: Sheed and Ward.

Futrell, John Carroll (1970a). *Making an Apostolic Community of Love: The Role of the Superior according to St. Ignatius of Loyola*. St. Louis: The Institute of Jesuit Sources.

——— (1970b). "Ignatian Discernment," 47–88 of *Studies in the Spirituality of the Jesuits,* Vol. II, No. 2 (April 1970).

——— (1972). "Communal Discernment: Reflections on Experience," 159–92 of *Studies in the Spirituality of the Jesuits,* Vol. IV, No. 5 (November 1972).

Ganss, George E. (1992). *The Spiritual Exercises of St Ignatius: a Translation and Commentary*. Chicago: Loyola University Press.

Godet, Michel (1999). "Scenarios and Strategies: A Toolbox for Scenario Planning," *LIPS Working Papers,* special issue 2nd edition, April 1999 (downloaded 3 July 05).

Goux-Baudiment, Fabienne (2001). "Measuring and Maximizing the Impact of Regional Foresight" in *The IPTS Report,* no. 59 (downloaded 3 July 05).

Green, Thomas H. (1984). *Weeds Among the Wheat: Discernment: Where Prayer and Action Meet*. Notre Dame, IN: Ave Maria Press.

Harrington, Wilfrid (2005). "Scribalism in the Church" 44–55 of Angela Hanley and David Smith (eds.) *Quench Not the Spirit: Theology and Prophecy for the Church in the Modern World*. Dublin: Columba.

Hertz, Noreena (2001). *The Silent Takeover: Global Capitalism and the Death of Democracy*. London: Heinemann.

Hope, Anne and Sally Timmel (1995). *Training for Transformation: A Handbook for Community Workers Vols. 1–3* (2nd revised ed.). Gweru, Zimbabwe: Mambo Press.

——— (1999). *Training for Transformation: A Handbook for Community Workers Vol. 4*. Kleinmond, South Africa: Training for Transformation Institute.

Howard, Sue and Welbourn, David (2004). *The Spirit at Work Phenomenon*. London: Azure.

Ignatius of Loyola: The Spiritual Exercises. See under Ganss, under Puhl, and under Fleming.

Ignatius of Loyola (1996). *Personal Writings*. London: Penguin Classics.

Lancaster, Judith and Philip Endean (eds.) (2004). *Cornelia Connelly and Her Interpreters*. London: The Way Publications.

Lonergan, Bernard (1972). *Method in Theology*. New York: Herder and Herder; London: Darton, Longman & Todd.

——— (1992). *Insight: A Study of Human Understanding* (Collected Works of Bernard Lonergan, Vol. 3). Toronto: University of Toronto Press (original edition 1957).

Markham, Donna J. (1999). *Spiritlinking Leadership: Working through Resistance to Organizational Change*. New York: Paulist.

Milbank, John (2005). "Liberality versus Liberalism" a paper delivered to the conference in Vatican City on "The Call to Justice: the Legacy of *Gaudium et Spes* Forty Years Later" March 2005, at http://www.stthomas.edu/gaudium/ (downloaded 27 May 2005).

Mills, John O. (1983). "Dominicans and Jesuits, September 1983," 180–91 of *Religious Life Review* (July–August 1983).

Mindell, Arnold (1995). *Sitting in the Fire: Large Group Transformation Using Conflict and Diversity*. Portland, Oregon: Lao Tse Press.

Morison, Samuel Eliot (1965). *The Oxford History of the American People*. New York: OUP.

Murphy, Lawrence (1976). "Consolation" 35–47 of *The Way Supplement* No. 27, (Spring 1976).

Murray, Pat (2005). Personal email giving her interpretation of Mary Ward's approach to authority.

Norton, Anne (2004). *Leo Strauss and the Politics of American Empire*. New Haven, CT: Yale.

O'Connell, Timothy E. (1998). Making Disciples: A Handbook of Christian Formation. New York: Crossroad Herder.

O'Dwyer, Malachy (2003). "Reclaiming the Dominican Vision for the 21st Century: Pursuing Communion in Government," 214–32 of *Religious Life Review* (July–August 2003).

Orchard, Gillian (ed.) (1985). Till God Will: Mary Ward through her writings: London: Darton, Longman & Todd.

Orsy, Ladislas (1973). "Towards a Theological Evaluation of Communal Discernment," 139–86 of *Studies in the Spirituality of the Jesuits*, Vol. V, No. 5 (October 1973).

Pearmain, Rosalind (2001). *The Heart of Listening: Attentional Skills in Psychotherapy.* London and New York: Continuum.

Puhl, Louis J. (1963). *The Spiritual Exercises of St. Ignatius: a New Translation Based on Studies in the Language of the Autograph.* Westminster, MD: The Newman Press.

Rahner, Karl (1964). "The Logic of Concrete Individual Knowledge in Ignatius Loyola," 84–170 of *The Dynamic Element in the Church.* Freiburg: Herder; London: Burns & Oates.

Toner, Jules J. (1971). "A Method for Communal Discernment of God's Will," 121–52 of *Studies in the Spirituality of the Jesuits*, Vol. III, No. 4 (September 1971).

——— (1974). "The Deliberation That Started the Jesuits," (iii)–(ix) and 179–212 of *Studies in the Spirituality of the Jesuits*, Vol. VI, No. 4 (June 1974).

——— (1982). *A Commentary on Saint Ignatius' Rules for the Discernment of Spirits.* St. Louis: Institute of Jesuit Sources.

——— (1991). *Discerning God's Will: Ignatius of Loyola's Teaching on Christian Decision Making.* St. Louis: Institute of Jesuit Sources.

——— (1995). *What Is Your Will, O God?* St. Louis: Institute of Jesuit Sources.

Tyrrell, Bernard J. (1996). "Affectional Conversion: A Distinct Conversion or Potential Differentiation in the Spheres of Sensitive Psychic and/or Affective Conversion?" 1–36 of *Method: Journal of Lonergan Studies* Vol. 14, No. 1 (Spring 1996).

Varley, Virginia (1996). "Fostering the Process of Discerning Together," 84–97 of *The Way Supplement* No. 85 (Spring 1996).

Verstraeten, Johan (2005). Lecture at Conference on Business Ethics in Milltown Park, Dublin, 23 September 2005; this lecture was based on material from his forthcoming book.

Vertin, Michael (1994). "Lonergan on Consciousness: Is there a fifth level?" 1–36 of *Method: Journal of Lonergan Studies* Vol. 12, No. 1 (Spring 1994).

Wright, Jonathan (2005). *The Jesuits: Missions, Myths and Histories*. London: Harper Perennial.

Index